A WORLD IN FLAMES
IN THE AIR

Peter Hepplewhite is an escaped history teacher, currently hiding in the cellars of Tyne and Wear Archives Service where he works as Education Officer. He has been a freelance writer for more than ten years, starting with school textbooks (boo!) before he realized that war stories were more thrilling.

A WORLD IN FLAMES
IN THE AIR

PETER HEPPLEWHITE

Illustrations and maps by David Wyatt

MACMILLAN CHILDREN'S BOOKS

To Addy, the aerial baby

First published 2001
by Macmillan Children's Books
a division of Pan Macmillan Limited
20 New Wharf Road, London N1 9RR
Basingstoke and Oxford
www.panmacmillan.com

Associated companies throughout the world

ISBN 0 330 48296 3

1 3 5 7 9 8 6 4 2

A CIP catalogue record for this book is available from the British Library.

Printed by Mackays of Chatham plc, Chatham, Kent.

CONTENTS

INTRODUCTION

In 1998 newspapers carried a strange report. A 71-year-old man drove his car into a ditch because he thought a passing plane was about 'to shoot him up'. A few weeks earlier he had suffered a terrifying nightmare for the first time. He was running headlong from German fighters that dived at him with guns blazing. And, as if that wasn't bad enough, when he tried to get away, he was pursued by a pack of fierce dogs.

Night after night the same terrible dream recurred and he woke sweating and exhausted. The only thing that would calm his mind was visiting a quiet field where he could hear the voices of long-dead friends. What on earth was happening to him? Slowly he told a psychiatrist his story.

The man was a veteran of World War II. He had watched German air raids pound British cities in the first few years of the war while he was a teenager, and made up his mind to strike back. When he was 18 he joined RAF Bomber Command and went on to fly 30 missions over Germany. In many of these he watched helplessly as other members of his crew were killed by enemy fighters or anti-aircraft fire.

On his last mission in December 1944 he parachuted from a burning plane and was captured by the Germans. Four months later he escaped, only to be hunted down by guards with dogs. For years he coped with the memories without too much difficulty – then suddenly they became too much to bear. Fifty years after World War II ended he was suffering from battle shock. He was still paying the price of the war in the air.

Many of this veteran's experiences were shared by over a million men and women who served in the RAF during the war. Those still alive are now in their late 70s or older. Their memories of events are mixed. The war was a time of achievement, friendship and excitement but also of sadness, death and destruction.

This book snapshots six stunning stories from that whirlwind time and gives you the fighting facts behind them.

- In 1940 Stuka dive-bombers pound a Sussex radar station. Will they blind Britain's electronic eyes and pave the way for a German invasion?
- As the Battle of Britain reaches its height a desperate Hurricane pilot runs out of ammunition. How

can he stop a German bomber heading straight for Buckingham Palace?

- Deadly Focke-Wulf fighters pounce on a Lancaster bomber over Berlin. Does the stricken plane stand a chance of ever making it home?
- Trapped by searing anti-aircraft fire, an American B-17 bomber bursts into flames. Will the courage of one crewman be enough to fight the fire?
- Blowing down the walls of Amiens prison and rescuing 700 Resistance fighters. Is this a mission impossible for the Mosquito squadrons?
- During the summer of 1944 a new weapon blasts London. Can Britain's best fighter pilots stop the sinister V1 flying bombs?

RADAR
WARNING

BATTLE BRIEFING

No Surrender

By the end of June 1940 German forces had conquered most of Western Europe. The British army had been defeated in France and had barely escaped from the wreckage-strewn beaches of Dunkirk. As the summer drew on Adolf Hitler, the German leader, expected the British to negotiate peace — that seemed the only sensible thing for them to do. But the British didn't see it that way. They rallied around their maverick Prime Minister, Winston Churchill, and fought on.

The Battle of Britain

On 16 July Hitler signed the order for Operation Sea Lion, the plan to invade southern England. But before the German army could cross the Channel, the Luftwaffe (the German air force) had to snatch control of the skies and wipe out the Royal Navy. In their way stood RAF Fighter Command. Churchill called this epic struggle for survival, 'the Battle of Britain'.

On Sunday 18 August, 1940, the Germans launched an air raid to punch a hole in Britain's radar network (see Fighting Facts) and 24-year-old WAAF (Women's Auxiliary Air Force) Corporal Joan Avis Hearn found herself in the front line ...

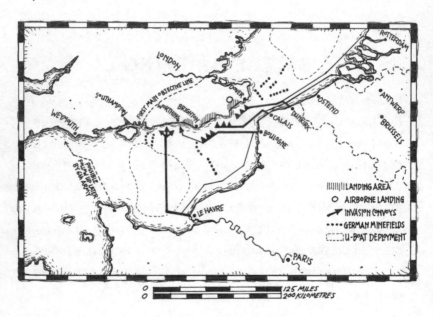

The plan for Operation Sea Lion.

THE STUKAS STRIKE

Dive-bombers

The Stukas were lined up proudly, ready for take-off. Thirty-two-year-old Major Helmut Bode was to lead the attack. He was in command of the 31 planes of Third Group, Dive Bomber Geschwader 77. Their target that afternoon was the 'radio station' at Poling, near Littlehampton in Sussex. He had not been told their true purpose – the 90 m high metal masts were, in fact, far more important. They were part of Britain's top-secret defence system – radar.

Helmut was confident. He knew the RAF would be a tough nut to crack, but he had no doubts that the Luftwaffe would win. Stukas had been the spearhead of the Nazi **Blitzkrieg** that had conquered Europe. Now it was time to bomb Britain into submission and Third Group were eager to play their part.

'Stuka' was the nickname for the Junkers 87, a shortened form of the German word for dive-bomber, Sturzkampfflugzeug. The Junkers was a strange-looking plane. With its bent wings and fixed undercarriage, it looked like a prehistoric bird. It was slow too, with a top speed of only 232 mph. But the Stuka was not designed to take on enemy fighters. It was a deadly precision bomber. Each aircraft was loaded with a 250 kg bomb under the **fuselage** and four 50 kg bombs under the wings. When the Stuka began its screaming dive, few targets survived intact.

At 12:30 exactly, Helmut opened his throttle wide and bumped across the grass airfield near Cherbourg. Fully laden, his plane lumbered slowly into the air. Poling was only 85 miles away, about 30 minutes' flying time. By 12:45 the rest of the Group was airborne and in formation around him. And they were not alone. Three other Stuka Groups, assigned to knock out coastal airfields, soon pulled alongside – a grand total of 111 dive-bombers. Minutes later, this air armada was complete, as an escort of around 55 Messerschmitt Bf 109 fighters swung into position above them. Helmut had the comforting thought that any Hurricanes or Spitfires that tried to interfere would get a rough reception.

Time to Duck

At Poling radar station, Joan Avis Hearn had gone on duty at 13:00. Joan was one of the first women to train as a radar operator and had been posted to Poling in December 1939. Radar was still top-secret and she had been warned not to talk about her work. She later recalled:

> The local people probably thought that our two tall radar masts – one for transmitting and one for receiving – were some kind of science fiction 'death ray'.

Service life for Joan had been a strange mixture of luxury and rough-and-tumble. Since there were no

WAAF Corporal Joan Avis Hearn.

RAF barracks at Poling, the WAAFs stayed at Arundel Castle. They shared a suite of rooms, with their own butler to serve them meals. In contrast, the station was little more than a series of wooden huts protected by sandbags. A new, blast-proof concrete bunker was almost finished but by the summer of 1940 only the telephone links had been moved into its protecting walls.

Shortly after Joan began her afternoon watch it

Aerial view of Dover.

became clear trouble was brewing. The Poling radar screens showed a big raid building up over France – Helmut Bode's Stukas! When Joan was ordered into the bunker to operate the telephone switchboard, she had a feeling of dread. Nearby stations at Rye, Pevensey and Ventnor had been bombed in previous days. Was it Poling's turn now she wondered.

Joan didn't have time to worry for long. Soon she was busy passing radar plots of enemy planes from Poling and other nearby stations to the Filter Room at Bentley Priory. There should have been two WAAFs handling the flow of calls but the station was shorthanded and she struggled on alone.

Suddenly at around 13:30, Sergeant Blundell rang through with an urgent message. 'Raiders, Joan! Time to duck.'

'Sorry, sir,' she replied, 'I can't leave yet, there's too much information coming in.'

Moments later an urgent voice came over the line from the nearby radar station at Truleigh Hill. 'Poling! Poling! Do you realize the last plot we've given you is right on top of you?'

And even as Joan listened, an eerie sound drowned out the warning – the scream of dive-bombers.

Stuka Attack

Four thousand metres overhead Helmut Bode dropped his Stuka into an 80-degree dive, fixing his sights on the target buildings.

At 485 kph he plunged 3,000 metres in less than 30 seconds. As he dropped he sprayed the radar station with machine-gun bullets. Woe betide any defenders who didn't keep their heads down.

At 1,000 metres a warning horn sounded – four seconds to bomb release.

At 700 metres the horn cut off and Helmut hit the release button on his control column.

As the bombs fell away an automatic pull-out system heaved the nose of the Stuka level with the horizon. The crushing return of gravity smashed him back, hard against his seat. On either side of Helmut two other Stukas went

Stukas diving to attack.

through the same drill at the same time. It was a unit ploy, always strike in threes to divide the fire of anti-aircraft guns. In less than five minutes the attack was over and Third Group were streaming back to France.

Tiny Heroine

At only four feet ten inches tall, Joan Avis Hearn was the smallest recruit in the RAF, but that afternoon she was to show the courage of a giant. As the dive-bombers screeched and bombs burst round the bunker, she pulled on a tin hat and stayed at her post. She believed that any information she got through to Bentley Priory might be vital in repelling the attack.

In the midst of the explosions a shocked and shaken Post Office engineer staggered in. It was his unlucky day. He had been installing new telephone lines when the raid began. Joan didn't show him much sympathy, however. She thrust a receiver into his hand and ordered, 'Repeat everything I say to you.'

Calmly Joan continued to read the plots from other radar stations while her reluctant ally passed the messages on. At the other end of the line, the Filter Room plotter could hear the bombs raining down. Her anxious questions echoed over the receiver. 'Poling, Poling, are you all right?'

For a short time the brave pair battled on, then the explosions came too close. A near-miss ripped the blast-proof door off its iron hinges and the telephone switchboard went berserk, with lights popping and bells ringing. Through clouds of dust and debris an officer burst in and ordered them to get out quickly. Joan emerged into a scene of chaos. Bode's Stukas had dropped over 80 bombs. Half of them had hit the station. She remembered a scene of devastation:

There were craters everywhere, the concrete aerial supports pitted by machine-gun bullets and the top of one of the masts shorn away. The lorry that brought us to Poling that morning was burning fiercely, and the officer's lovely Lagonda sports car was a gutted wreck. Our only defence was a Lewis gun (machine-gun) manned by an army detachment whose billet was a mass of flames.

*On reflection the arrival of the Post Office engineer
probably saved my life. If he hadn't turned up, I might
have been tempted to run for it. I wouldn't have stood
a chance ...*

Counting the Cost

On the way home Helmut Bode's pilots escaped lightly.
RAF Hurricanes and Spitfires pounced but only one
Stuka was shot down, while a second crash-landed in
France. Their comrades were not so fortunate. Other
units had been harder hit, especially First Group during
their attack on Thorny Island airfield. The **Luftwaffe**
War Diaries later counted the cost:

*Of its 28 aircraft twelve failed to return and six others
were so shot up that they only just made it back to
France. Adding the casualties of the other Groups, 30
Junkers 87s were either lost or severely damaged. The
price was too high.*

After this bruising day, Stukas were considered too
vulnerable to face RAF fighters. They were not used in
large numbers again during the Battle of Britain.

In spite of the destruction Joan had seen at Poling,
the radar station was only partly damaged. The long-
range radar was out of action until the end of August,
but the system for detecting low-flying aircraft was
quickly in action again. Mobile transmitters were set up
in caravans in the nearby Angmering woods and only

two days later picked up the plots of another large raid.

Still nervous, Joan was delighted to see the German formations smashed by the RAF before they got close. The Luftwaffe had failed to wreck Britain's invisible shield.

On 22 March 1941, Joan Avis Hearn was awarded the Military Medal by King George VI at Buckingham Palace. When the King asked about her work, she carefully replied that she was a telephone operator. After all, radar was hush-hush and no one had told her if His Majesty knew about it. If he didn't, she wasn't going to let the cat out of the bag.

FIGHTING FACTS

The Winning Formula

German Plans: The Luftwaffe had to gain 'air superiority' (control of the air) over southern England so that the German invasion fleet could cross the Channel safely.

Objective 1

Bomb targets such as airfields and factories to force the RAF to protect them with Spitfires and Hurricanes. Catch and destroy these modern fighters, leaving Britain without air defence.

Objective 2

With the British fighters out of the way, use bombers to sink the Royal Navy.

The Luftwaffe wanted Fighter Command to slug it out for command of the air, like two heavy-weight boxers – winner takes all!

Order from Herman Goering, Commander-in-Chief of the Luftwaffe, 19 August, 1940: *Inflict the utmost possible damage on enemy fighter forces.*

British Plans: The Head of Fighter Command was Air Chief Marshal, Sir Hugh Dowding. He realized that to win the battle of Britain his force of some 700 Hurricane and Spitfire planes had to hold out against over 1,500 German bombers and 1,100 fighters. Winning did not mean destroying the Luftwaffe but making sure enough fighters survived to protect the Royal Navy – and make a German invasion too risky.

Order from Air Vice-Marshall Keith Park, Commander of No. 11 Group, 19 August 1940: *Our main object is to engage enemy bombers.*

Radar Evens the Odds

If the RAF knew how many enemy planes were coming – and if they could attack them at the right place, the right time and the right height – their chances of winning would be much greater. Fortunately, from 1936, Dowding had backed a high-tech defence system that gave exactly this information – radar.

Death Ray Experiments

Have passing planes ever caused interference on your radio – just when that crucial goal of the match is about to be scored the sound is drowned by static? When radio broadcasts began in the 1920s it was noticed that signals were often disrupted by aircraft. This led to some wild ideas:

Wild Idea 1

Electromagnetic waves might kill the aircrew of enemy planes – a death ray.

Wild Idea 2

High-powered radio waves might be used to detonate bombs on board an enemy aircraft before it reached its target.

Weird! But interesting enough for the Air Ministry to pay for more research. In 1935 Robert Watson-Watt, head of Radio Research at the National Physical Laboratory, investigated and dismissed these theories as science fiction. However he did have a practical idea:

Common-sense Idea

Watson-Watt proved that radio waves could be used to detect aircraft by measuring the time it took for a signal to bounce back from a plane. It was the start of four years of hectic work.

By 1939 the east coast of Britain was guarded by two radar systems:

1. the Chain Home stations that detected planes 100 miles away, and
2. the Chain Home Low stations that located aircraft flying under 1,000 m.

Chain home radar towers.

Radar Control

Both radar systems fed their information by telephone to the Filter Room at Fighter Command Headquarters at Bentley Priory, in Middlesex. The Filter Room was a telephone exchange where the information was collated and cross-checked before it was sent to the Operations

The filter room at RAF Fighter Command Headquarters,
Bentley Priory.

Room. Here a giant map and 'ops' table displayed aircraft tracks over the whole of Britain and the sea approaches. This gave Dowding and his commanders a complete picture of each day's battles.

The British 'Few'

On 20 August 1940 Winston Churchill praised the pilots of Fighter Command and called them 'the few' who 'are turning the tide of war'. Although they were only a tiny part of a huge war effort by tens of thousands of people, the Battle of Britain was won by the skill and courage of 3,080 pilots. Sadly, 515 of these were killed. Although the majority were British, many airmen of different nationalities also served – and almost 100 of them died.

Fighter Command – The Few

Nationality	Number of Pilots	Number Killed
British	2,543	478
Polish	147	30
New Zealand	101	14
Canadian	94	20
Czech	87	8
Belgian	29	6
South African	22	9
Australian	22	9
French	14	0
Irish	10	1
American	7	1
Southern Rhodesian	2	0
Jamaican	1	0
Palestinian	1	0
Total	**3,080**	**515**

The German 'Few'

The Luftwaffe Messerschmitt (Me) 109 fighter pilots could not be blamed if they also thought of themselves as 'the few'. Certainly, if bombers are included, the

Main German aircraft in the Battle of Britain

Type	Max. Speed	Range	Weapons	Comment
Messerschmitt 109E, single-engined fighter. Nicknamed the 'Emil'.	357 mph (576 kph) at 12,300 ft (3,750 m)	410 miles (660 km)	Twin machine-guns in the fuselage and two 20 mm cannon in the wings.	The equal of the Spitfire and armed with cannon.
Messerschmitt 110, twin-engined fighter. Nicknamed 'the destroyer'.	336 mph (541 kph) at 19,685 ft (6,000 m)	565 miles (910 km) Able to reach almost all of England and Wales from northern France.	Two 20 mm cannon and four small calibre machine-guns.	One of the best twin-engined fighters in the world, but no match for Hurricanes or Spitfires.
Junkers Ju 87 'Stuka', dive-bomber.	238 mph (380 kph) with bomb load at 13,410 ft (4,085 m)	370 miles (595 km)	Three machine-guns, two firing forwards, one backwards. Bomb load of about 500 kg.	A very accurate bomber but slow and vulnerable to fighters
Junkers Ju 88, twin-engined bomber.	224 mph (448 kph) with bomb load at 18,050 ft (5,055 m)	1,055 miles (1,700 km) with extra fuel tank.	Four hand-held machine-guns. Bomb load of 2,000 kg.	Good as either a horizontal or a dive-bomber.
Dornier Do17, twin-engined bomber. Nicknamed the 'flying pencil'.	224 mph (360 kph) with bomb load at 13,120 ft	720 miles (1,160 km) with bomb load and extra fuel tank.	Four hand-held machine-guns. Bomb load of 1,000 kg.	The Dornier's air-cooled engines were less vulnerable to enemy fire.
Heinkel He 111P, twin-engined bomber.	247 mph (395 kph) with bomb load at 16,400 ft (5,000 m)	1,224 miles (1,960 km) with bomb load and extra fuel tank.	Five to seven machine-guns. Bomb load of 2,000 kg.	The most numerous German bomber during the Battle of Britain but also the most vulnerable.

attacking German air force greatly outnumbered Fighter Command. But the most important fighting was between Hurricanes, Spitfires and Me 109s.

At the beginning of the Battle of Britain the Luftwaffe had about 725 109s ready for action – almost the same number of fast, single-engined fighters as the RAF. On 1 September this number had fallen to 438 and by 1 October to 275.

WAAFs at War

The Women's Auxiliary Air Force was set up in June 1939. At the time of the Battle of Britain women were limited to half a dozen RAF trades, including cooks, drivers, telephonists and barrage balloon fabric repairers. And then there were the clerks (special duty) – a boring name which hid front-line action during the summer of 1940. These were the women who manned the ops rooms, radio interception stations and radar stations – women like Joan.

Listening to the Enemy

One of the best-kept secrets of the war was the 'Y (Interception) Service'. WAAFs who could speak German monitored radio transmissions, and by listening carefully to the 'chatter' of German pilots were able to build up a picture of the Luftwaffe Order of Battle – a detailed list of the units attacking Britain and where they were based. Horribly, they also listened to the sound of

WAAF recruiting poster.

men dying in their planes. Section Officer Aileen Morris remembered:

There were occasions when we would intercept a message from a German formation approaching RAF fighters ... having spotted our aircraft before they themselves were observed. We were then likely to hear: Indianer unten fuenf Uhr, Kirchturm 4, Aufpassen *(Bandits below at five o'clock, height 5,000 m, look out). In those days we were unable to get through in time for it to be of use, and would get hopping mad that we had no means of warning our fighters that they were about to be jumped.*

Then Angreifen (attack) the formation leader would yell, and we would know that the German fighters were diving on their target. I would hear one of the RAF monitors murmuring: 'Oh God ... oh God ... please ... please ... look up ...' and I knew how helpless she felt.

There was sympathy too for the Germans. A WAAF sergeant at Hawkinge airfield in Kent was used to hearing a cheery-sounding Luftwaffe pilot as he made regular reconnaissance trips over the Channel. Then, one day, he was shot down in flames by Spitfires. She recalled:

He was unable to get out and we listened to him as he screamed and screamed for his mother and cursed Hitler. I found myself praying, 'Get out, bale out, oh please, dear God, get him out.' But it was no use. We heard him all the way down until he fell below reception range. I went out and was sick.

The Battle Goes On
The day of the attack on Poling saw the hardest fighting in the Battle of Britain. The Luftwaffe lost 71 planes and the RAF 27. But the struggle was far from over. The make or break day for the Luftwaffe was to be 15

September – remembered since as Battle of Britain Day. As you will see in the next tense chapter, Hurricane pilot Ray Holmes was in the thick of the action.

BATTLE OF BRITAIN DAY

BATTLE BRIEFING

The Blitz Begins

On 7 September 1940 the Luftwaffe began raids on London. This was the start of the Blitz – 76 nights of non-stop terror bombing. During this first attack German bombers escaped almost unscathed. RAF flight controllers had mistakenly sent their fighters to protect airfields to the north and east of the capital. It would not happen again. In the days that followed the Luftwaffe paid a heavy price.

On 15 September radar reported the largest German formations yet seen heading for London. The twelve Hurricanes of 504 Squadron, based at RAF Hendon, were among the fighters waiting for them ...

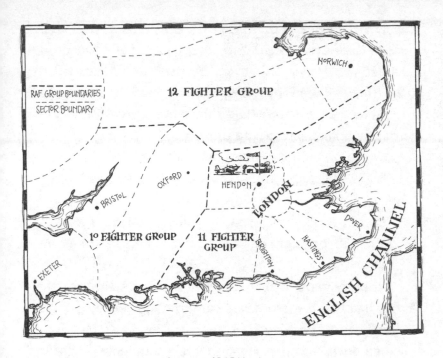

Location of RAF Hendon.

SAVE THE PALACE

A Long Morning

Sergeant Ray T. Holmes, 'Arty' to his mates, sighed as he stepped into a hot bath. 'What a maddening time it has been,' he thought crossly as he looked at his watch. 'Almost 11 o'clock. Where are the Luftwaffe? What is going on? We've been ready for take-off since sun-up.' As he lay back and began to relax, his mind flicked back over the events of that trying morning.

It had begun with the usual early start. At 05:00, still in darkness, Arty and the other pilots of 504 Squadron had stumbled out of bed and dressed. Still bleary-eyed they had climbed into the Humber truck, that carried them to their planes. While they were driven round the airfield perimeter track the usual rude banter began.

'Own up, who peed in my shoe last night?'

'Sorry, old chap, I couldn't wait. You know how far the toilet is.'

'It's not good enough, pee in your own damn shoe.'

'Well, if you feel like that about it I'll use someone else's ...'

Nobody minded that this was the same silly prattle they had heard yesterday ... and the day before ... and every day since they had been stationed at Hendon. When death was peering over their shoulders, laughter was precious.

By the time they arrived at **dispersal** they were awake and chirpy. It was just as well. The next job was the careful inspection of their planes and equipment. It was the same vital routine every dawn.

CHECK: helmet, parachute and map.
CHECK: fuel, guns and radio.
CHECK: engines, hydraulics and electrics.

When he fought the enemy at 300 mph (480 kph), 15,000 feet (4,570 m) above the ground, the last thing Arty wanted was a blunder that should have been spotted on the ground. His ground crew were superb, but it was comforting to know he had looked over things himself.

With the inspections finished the commanding officer (CO) had reported to Group Command that 504 Squadron were ready for action. Then the waiting began. In the flight hut – a crew hut with basic facilities: toilets, kettle, chairs, telephone – the pilots brewed tea and passed the nerve-wracking time as best they could. Some played poker or read the newspapers, while others gratefully went back to sleep, curled up on mattresses on the crew room floor.

As the sun climbed, the day promised to be warm and clear, beautiful late summer weather. Perfect for bombers! Yet, as the morning shuffled slowly by, the radar stations showed no sign of a German attack. Finally the squadron was told to stand down. Half relieved and half disappointed, the pilots were driven back to the Officers' Mess. Tired and scruffy from his early start, Arty headed for the bathroom. And there he was, in a steaming tub, wondering what on earth had happened to the war.

Scramble
Suddenly a loud rap on the door interrupted his thoughts.

'Quick, Ray, there's a flap on – we're on readiness again!'

(Readiness – ready to take off within five minutes.)

Cursing to himself, Arty leapt out of the bath. Without pausing to dry he squirmed into his uniform and ran for the truck, socks in hand. He was still struggling to pull them on when they screeched up to the flight hut.

It was 11:15 and the order to scramble had just come over the telephone from the Sector HQ at North Weald. As he announced this over the loudspeakers, the duty operator leaned over to the gramophone and put the squadron 'Scramble Song 'on the turntable. While Arty rushed to his locker and pulled on his life jacket and boots, the William Tell Overture blared out:

Diddle-um, diddle-um, diddle-um pom, pom.

Diddle-um, diddle-um, diddle-um pom, pom.

It was a 504 squadron joke: 'William Tell, run like hell.' The rousing music gave the pilots a buzz as they hurried to take off.

By the time Arty had sprinted to his Hurricane, the ground crew had started the roaring Merlin engine. In a blur of activity they helped him into the cockpit and parachute harness. His helmet was already plugged into the radio and oxygen supply as he rammed it over his bedraggled hair.

Waving chocks away, Arty taxied across the bumpy grass airstrip to the far end of the field. Hendon was a small station surrounded by houses and the Hurricanes needed every inch they could get to clear the rooftops. With the wind behind them and throttles rammed open the squadron soared into the air in an untidy gaggle. Had enemy fighters jumped them, they would have been helpless.

Once airborne, 504 formed up into A and B flights, two parallel lines of six planes. Arty was at the back in charge of Green section, B flight. They were the weavers, the rear guard, keeping look-out behind. Soon instructions came over the radio to climb to 17,000 feet and intercept a raid of 30 or more bombers closing in on London from the south-east.

Within minutes they were in sight, like a flock of seagulls in the distance. (German bombers flew in a V formation – a leader and two **wingmen**.) But they were coming up fast – Dornier 17s in a tight, disciplined formation. Arty quickly recognized their sinister shape – the large glass nose, looking angry and swollen compared to the slim fuselage and fragile-looking twin tail. 'Ugly beggars,' he thought.

'Tally Ho!'

Abruptly the radio crackled into life, 'Tally Ho!' The enemy had been sighted. As each Hurricane swooped in, the pilots picked their targets and opened fire. By the time Arty piled in from the back of the group the sky was already a crazy jumble of wheeling and jostling aircraft.

Although the German bombers were slow, they were far from helpless. Flying through a fierce barrage, Arty got a Dornier in the orange circle of his sights. He pushed hard on the gun button and his plane shook as the eight Browning machine-guns spat out a storm of bullets. Even a short burst was enough to rip through an enemy aircraft, and it was important not to waste bullets. Hurricanes only carried enough ammunition for 14 seconds firing time.

Air combat was fast and furious. A pilot who needed time to think, 'What do I do now?' would not last long. That was why so many rookie pilots were shot down on their first mission. But Arty was a survivor. Even as he pressed his gun button he was ready for the next problem – breaking off the attack safely. If he overshot the bomber he would expose the vulnerable belly of his Hurricane to the German gunners. Instead, the split second he stopped firing, he banked sharply left and dived steeply.

As his plane dropped, Arty checked to make sure no one was on his tail. Good, all clear. He breathed deeply to ease the fierce pressure crushing his chest and levelled out. Now it was time to climb back into the fight. But what fight? As he scanned the sky above it was empty. His dive had carried him out of sight of the dozens of raging planes . . . or had it? As he glanced west, he saw three Dorniers in a tight V formation. He guessed they were the original leaders of the German bomber group, still on course for London. And since there were no other British fighters in sight, he would have to stop them!

Arty opened the throttle and raced after the Dorniers, a plan already forming in his mind. Charge up from behind, guns blazing? No that would be suicide – a mad rush into the tracks of their rear guns. A flanking manoeuvre to take out the port wingman? Much better! Moving almost as fast as thought, Arty crabbed in at an angle, so that his target shielded him from the fire of the other bombers.

It worked. He opened fire at 400 yards and smoke soon engulfed the Hurricane. The bomber was hit. Wait! This wasn't smoke. It was oil. Thick black oil right across his canopy. He couldn't see a blinking thing. Blind! Instinctively he shut the throttle and prayed. Even so, in the moments it took for the air stream to blast the oil free Arty came close to disaster. When his vision cleared, a huge shape blotted out the sky. It was the Dornier, slowing down fast – and he was about to ram into it. Desperately Arty shoved the control lever forward, so fiercely that he felt the shoulder straps of his safety harness bite into his collarbone. With inches to spare the Hurricane ducked under the bomber, barely escaping the propellers.

As the stricken bomber glided slowly downwards, Arty turned his attention to the remaining pair. He would go for the other wingman first. Swinging over to the starboard side he roared forward and closed in for another attack. His first burst was bang on target and flames rippled down the Dornier. Suddenly there was a flicker of white! Someone trying to bale out? Then Arty lost control, the Hurricane was heaving about like a mad creature. Fighting the stick he levelled his plane and anxiously looked for damage. No. It couldn't be! Incredibly a German was hanging from his port wing, trapped by his parachute canopy.

Arty had never really thought about the enemy he hunted every day. They were invaders, but the battles were nothing personal. Just kill or be killed. Suddenly this poor devil was dangling from his wing at over 250 mph. He had to help him. He jerked the joystick from side to side, waggling the wings, but nothing happened. Something more violent was needed. Using hard right rudder he slewed the plane to starboard. Slowly at first, then in a flash, the parachute slid along the wing edge and dropped away.

There was no time to see if it opened cleanly, or if the German plummeted to his death – the third Dornier was still heading for central London. Arty was worried. Why hadn't the pilot turned to run for France? Only one bomber left out of more than 30. It was reckless to carry on alone. Was this Nazi on a suicide mission? Buckingham Palace had been hit a few days before, but no one had been hurt. Was he trying to finish off the Royal family? And if his bombs missed the Palace, what about the innocent civilians who might be killed?

Another splatter of oil smeared Arty's canopy. Only a little, but it set his heart pounding. This wasn't German oil. It was coming from the Hurricane. His plane had been hit too. As its lifeblood seeped away the Merlin engine began to run roughly, the rev counter surging. How long before it seized up? He had to act now before he was forced to land.

Ignoring the warning growls from the engine he opened the throttle and tore past the Dornier – only to turn and face it, almost but not quite, head on. A frontal attack was the best of all. It took nerves of steel, but gave him the chance to fire at point-blank range into the enemy cockpit. As the two planes closed in at over 500 mph Arty hit the gun button. The Brownings drummed ... and died. He was out of ammo.

A wave of dismay swept over Arty. In seconds he would have to break away to avoid a collision and the bomber would escape ... unless? ... Unless? The German tail-plane looked thin and weak. Almost before he had the idea Arty aimed his left wing at the nearest fin. The Hurricane was a tough kite, renowned for the punishment it could take. He would knock this Dornier for six, like a footballer tripping an opponent.

Crunch! Yet not much of a crunch. Amazing! He'd got away with it. The Hurricane dipped and he moved the control lever to correct it. Nothing! The nose fell. Arty jerked the control lever left and right. Again nothing. The plane was plunging straight down. Elation turned to shock. Far from getting away with it, the gallant aircraft was finished, all control gone.

Arty's Hurricane and a Dornier collide in mid-air.

Bale Out

In seconds the Hurricane had dropped almost 8,000 feet, tearing towards the ground at over 400 mph. Time to bail out! This was his first time for real, but Arty knew the drill. He unlocked and slid back the hood, undid the safety harness and heaved himself out of his seat. His head and body thrust into a thunderous vortex. The buffeting was so hard that at first he thought he had been sucked into the propeller. Yet something held him tight. He had forgotten to unplug the radio lead to his helmet.

With every instinct screaming, NO! NO! he struggled back into the cockpit and freed the lead. But fate had decided to play with Arty. As he fought his way out a second time, a blast jammed him backwards over the fuselage and snagged his parachute inside the cockpit. He knew that he was tearing towards the earth and kicked frantically against the control column. Suddenly the Hurricane began to spin and he was clear, thrown out by centrifugal force. He was clear, but clear did not mean safe.

As he shot out into the air, the tail of the plane clipped Arty's shoulder. He barely felt the blow, was only vaguely aware that his right arm and shoulder had gone numb; hardly realized he had been hurt – until he tried to pull the ripcord of his parachute. Arty's fingers closed over the D-ring, but he had no strength to tug it. Urgently he gripped his right wrist with his left hand and jerked. For what seemed an age nothing happened and then there was an explosion above him. The chute opened so hard that his boots flew off.

As Arty gazed upwards he could see the Dornier falling in lazy spirals, with the whole tail section sheared off. No wonder his plane had been damaged by the impact. Glancing down he could see the Hurricane about to slam into – my God! Central London. He was stunned to find he was only a few hundred feet over Victoria Station. His lone battle had been above thick cloud and he had not known that the last bomber had reached its target area.

With horror, Arty saw he was dropping straight towards a maze of electrified railway lines. Losing height rapidly, he pulled the rigging and veered towards a three-storey block of flats. If luck was on his side, he might just drift over them and land in the road ... THWACK! No luck. He hit the ridge tiles.

At first the chute billowed up, giving enough lift to support his weight. For a few shaky seconds he balanced on the slates, like a mad puppet. Then the chute collapsed and he slipped and rolled. With the edge looming, Arty scrabbled frantically for a hand-hold. After all he had been through it seemed he might break his neck falling off a roof.

With a last gasp, he grabbed at the guttering ... missed ... and toppled over. He hadn't time to scream before a wrenching jolt stopped his fall. Looking down he saw both legs were inside an empty dustbin. Looking up he saw his parachute wrapped around the top of the drainpipe. He was safe. His only injuries were his shoulder ... and his dignity.

A Home Guard Sergeant escorted Arty to see what was left of his Hurricane. It had come down at a crossroads and miraculously missed nearby buildings. The plane had plunged 5 m into the ground.

FIGHTING FACTS

Arty and the Flame Thrower

Years later Arty found out that on that late summer Sunday he had almost been the victim of a German secret weapon. Remember the oil that covered his canopy, blinding him? It wasn't from the damaged engine of a Dornier, the plane had been carrying an experimental flame thrower. The oil should have ignited and burned him to death.

What about the Germans?
The Dornier that Arty rammed was the first German aircraft brought down over central London. The crew survived – they bailed out, landing in the Oval cricket ground. The bomber crashed into Victoria Station.

Last Push by Luftwaffe
In the week after the first mass raid on London the Germans sensed victory.

Score Line
On 11 and 14 of September, Fighter Command and Luftwaffe losses were almost the same:

11 September – Score Line
Great Britain	29
Germany	25

14 September – Score Line
Great Britain	14
Germany	14

Better still, German pilots reported scrappy attacks by the RAF. Was this the collapse they had been expecting for weeks? Goering hoped that one more push would finish the job.

15 September

Morning Mayhem

Around 10:50 radar blips showed a big raid building up over the French coast. Amazingly the Germans spent half an hour sorting their formations out – 100 bombers, escorted by 400 Me 109 fighters. This gave ample time for the RAF to prepare a warm welcome.

The enemy planes were harried from the moment they crossed the coast, all the way to London. The climax of the battle came just before noon. Four squadrons of Hurricanes attacked the bombers (including Arty's 504 Squadron) while the famous pilot, Douglas Bader, who had lost his legs earlier in the war and flew with artificial limbs, led a 'Big Wing' of five squadrons of Spitfires against the Me 109s. This was a total of 60 planes. Many of the raiders simply dumped their bombs and turned for home.

Afternoon Anger

The British pilots had barely time to snatch a cup of tea and a bully beef sandwich before they were in the air again. A second attack came in at 14:00 – around 150 bombers and 300 fighters. This time, the Luftwaffe armada was hit by 170 RAF fighters over Kent. Above the hop fields, the sky became thick with the plumes of whirling dogfights as the 109s fought to protect the bombers.

Then, as the German planes neared the southern outskirts of London the battle became a rout. Just as the 109s were running out of fuel and turning for France, another twelve Squadrons of Hurricanes and Spitfires roared into sight. Stunned, most of the bomber pilots took the only sensible action to avoid a bloodbath – they dropped their bombs at random and ran.

15 September – Score Line

Fighter Command shot down   61
Luftwaffe shot down   29

Sea Lion Sunk

On the day when Luftwaffe pilots believed they had come to finish off the 'last fifty Spitfires', they found themselves facing over 300 fighters. It was clear that Fighter Command was far from beaten. Forty-eight hours later, Hitler postponed Operation Sea Lion, until 1941 at the earliest. Although enemy raids lasted until the end of October, 15 September is seen as the day the RAF won – 'Battle of Britain Day'.

Hurricane – The Forgotten Plane

The sleek Spitfire usually steals the glory in histories of the Battle of Britain. The Spitfire was the faster plane, but more than half the fighting was done by Hurricanes,

Fighter Command Aircraft during the Battle of Britain

Type	Max. Speed	Range	Weapons	Comment
Hawker Hurricane Mk I	324 mph (520 kph) at 15,650 ft	505 miles (815 km)	Eight .303 inch machine-guns in the wings.	Pilots liked the Hurricane because it could take a lot of punishment and still get them home.
Supermarine Spitfire Mk IA	365 mph (585 kph) at 19,000 ft (5,790 m)	575 miles (925 km)	Eight .303 inch machine-guns in the wings.	The perfect fighter combining grace, speed, flexibility and firepower.
Boulton Paul Defiant	304 mph at 17,000 ft (490 kph) 17,000 ft (5,180 m)	465 miles (750 km)	Four .303 inch machine-guns in a turret behind the cockpit.	Only two squadrons were equipped with Defiants during the battle and they took heavy losses.
Bristol Blenheim, twin-engined fighter	278 mph (475 kph) at 15,000 ft (4,570 m)	1,050 miles (1,690 km)	Five machine-guns firing forward and one in the rear turret.	Six squadrons of Blenheim light bombers were converted to fighters.

designed by Sydney Camm at Hawker Engineering. The prototype made its first flight in 1935, reaching a speed of 315 mph (505 kph) at 16,000 feet (4,875 m). By September 1939 the RAF had 500 Hurricanes in service. Like the Spitfire, the heart of the Hurricane was the powerful Rolls Royce Merlin engine. In July 1940, three out of five of the 700 RAF fighters were Hurricanes.

Bad Landings

Many pilots during the Battle of Britain faced their worst nightmare – being shot down. For some this meant death or capture – while others had amazing escapes and were back in action within a few days.

Trapped!

On 9 July, New Zealander Flight Lieutenant Al Deere had a narrow escape. During a dogfight over the Channel he collided with an Me 109. Astonishingly both planes survived but Al's Spitfire was badly damaged. He remembered, 'the force of the impact pitched me violently forward on to my cockpit harness, the straps of which bit viciously into my shoulders. At the same moment, the control column was snatched abruptly from my gripping fingers.' As smoke poured into the cockpit Al tried to bale out, only to find that the hood would not release. Trapped, he had no choice but to try an emergency landing – before he burned to death. Trailing clouds of smoke and flame he headed for the coast and crashed into a cornfield. Fear then gave him almost superhuman strength. With his bare hands, he smashed a hole in the Perspex canopy and clawed his way out.

Al led a charmed life. On 15 August he was shot down and baled out over Deal. Two weeks later, on 31 August, he was taking off from Hornchurch when a bomb burst near his Spitfire and blew it over. He wrote:

To this day I am not exactly clear what happened next. What I do remember is the impact with the ground and a terrifying period of ploughing along the ground upside down.

Bandaged and battered, Al was back in action the next day.

Shooting Pilots

On 15 August, Australian Hurricane pilot Johnny Cock of 87 Squadron, was hit over the sea near Portsmouth. Fellow pilot Denis David watched angrily as an Me 109 tried to kill him in mid-air as he baled out. Denis remembered:

His parachute cords went ping! ping! ping! – beginning to separate him from his chute canopy – as the bullets flew around him. I managed to get behind the murderous Hun and shoot him down. I circled Johnny till he hit the water …

The bodies of several RAF pilots who baled out were recovered riddled with bullets. One case was 'Wilkie' Wilkinson of 266 Squadron. He collided with a 109 on 18 August and, according to witnesses, he baled out and seemed unhurt. Yet when his body was found it was full of bullet holes. In spite of this, British airmen did not fire at enemy pilots who were parachuting to safety. However, the RAF slate was not completely clean.

Fighter Command pilots were under orders to shoot down German rescue seaplanes – even if they were plucking Luftwaffe aircrew from the Channel. Worse, Polish and Czech pilots, who deeply hated the Germans, could not be stopped from taking pot shots whenever they had the chance.

German and British Pilots' Jargon

Luftwaffe Language

Bleat – open fire with a machine gun

Cannon – an ace pilot

Crew – flying family

Dismount hot – to be shot down in flames

Eggs – bombs

Emil – Messerschmitt 109E fighter

Glow worms – searchlights

Indians – enemy aircraft

Measles – anti-aircraft fire

Rabbit – stupid officer

Tommies – British

RAF Jargon

Angels – height at which to fly in thousands of feet

Bandits – enemy aircraft identified

Bogey – unidentified aircraft

Crumpet – girl

Dogfight – air battle

Jerries – Germans

Readiness – combat ready to take off within five minutes

Scramble – take off at once

Shiners – barrage balloons

Tally ho – target sighted

Vector – turn on to specified course

BOMBERS OVER BERLIN

BATTLE BRIEFING

Bomber Command

Even before the Battle of Britain was over Winston Churchill wanted to hit back against Nazi-dominated Europe. But how was this to be done? The British had no allies left on the continent, and their army was no match for German troops. This left only one way of taking the fighting to the enemy – bombers.

In the early months of the war RAF Bomber Command was equipped with slow, twin-engined planes – Whitleys, Wellingtons and Hampdens. They could only deliver small bomb loads and suffered heavy losses to German fighters during daylight raids. Switching to night attacks cut casualties but brought other problems. Photographs showed that most bombs missed and were doing little damage to *the factories and transport systems that were the main targets.*

It was not until 1942 that Bomber Command became a real threat. A tough new Commanding Officer, Air Marshall Arthur 'Bomber' Harris took over to carry out a ruthless war aim. His orders from the government were blunt:

The primary objective of your operations is to break the **morale** of the civilian population, and in particular of the industrial workers ... the aiming points are to be the built-up areas, not for instance, the dockyards or aircraft factories.

In reality this meant: bomb German cities into the ground. In British eyes this was only equal to the savage Luftwaffe raids on London, Liverpool, Coventry and dozens of other towns. The Germans would reap what they had sown.

A range of new weapons and inventions were coming on stream to do the job. The mighty, four-engined Avro Lancaster could carry loads of up to 14,000 lb (6,350 kg) over a range of 1,040 miles (1,673 km). And Harris was promised a fleet of 4,000 bombers to reduce Germany to rubble. Hitting targets remained a problem but a series of devices helped. The 'Gee' radio navigation system guided raids to the target area while the H2S airborne radar set gave a map-like picture of the ground below.

In May 1942 1,047 bombers devastated Cologne. In 90 minutes 2,500 fires burnt out 3,330 buildings, killing 469 people and making 45,000 more homeless. Soon many

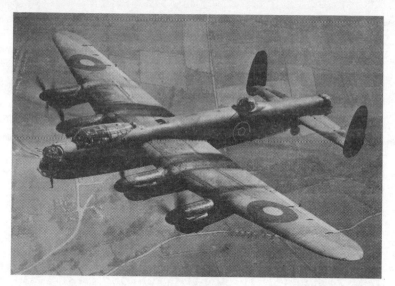

An Avro Lancaster.

other German cities were burning too – Dusseldorf, Essen, Frankfurt, Hamburg, Lubeck, Rostock.

In 1943–44, as Bomber Command grew in strength and confidence, the main target became the German capital – Berlin! The name was enough to make experienced bomber crews wince. A mission to 'The Big City' meant big trouble. Berlin was deep inside Germany, so deep that raiders could only be sure of getting there and back in the dark on long winter nights. It was heavily defended too – anti-aircraft guns and searchlights ringed the city, while night fighters prowled the black skies. The brave airmen went into action knowing that many of them would not be coming home again.

TARGET BERLIN

The evening of 15 February 1944 was cold and overcast. In this cheerless gloom, 891 heavily loaded Lancaster and Halifax bombers prepared for take-off. RAF Bomber Command had been fighting the 'Battle of Berlin' since November 1943. This was the fifteenth raid of the winter and would be the heaviest. It was one more step in the relentless plan to pound the German capital to ruins – the RAF attacking by night and the American air force, the USAF, by day.

Slowly, like lumbering ducks, the bombers reached take-off speed – 110 mph (175 kph) and clawed their way into the air. The throb of Merlin engines echoed for miles around dozens of aerodromes dotted across the eastern side of England. It took well over an hour for all

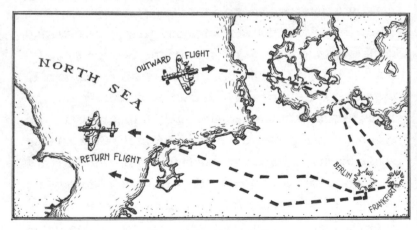

The routes to and from Berlin.

the planes to get airborne and even longer for them to climb into formation. In thousands of nearby homes families glanced at one another as they huddled close to their cosy fires. They knew what the distant roar meant. The cheerful Air Force 'lads' they met in the local shop or pub were going to war. Many comforted themselves with the thought, 'Jerry's going to get a pasting.' Yet what would be the cost? Which faces would be missing the following day?

That night's route took the Main Force out over the North Sea, across southern Denmark and the Baltic before swinging abruptly south to Berlin. It meant a gruelling eight-hour return flight. Another 24 Lancasters headed for Frankfurt-on-Oder, a diversion to draw off some of the German night fighters. But the enemy was not to be fooled. At 18:16 the first British bombers were picked up by German radar. Soon the whole bomber stream, spread over 80 miles of sky, showed clearly on the screens. With ample warning, the deadly Focke-Wulf 190s and Junker 88s were waiting.

Aussie Air Gunner

Lancaster ND444 GT-O of 156 Pathfinder Squadron had taken off from Warboys airfield in Cambridgeshire at 17:26. (7,377 Lancasters were built during the war, each with its own registration number. Most, unlike the American planes, were not given names by their crews.) Londoner Flight Sergeant Ken Doyle was in the pilot seat and Australian Flight Sergeant Geoffrey C. C. Smith was rear gunner. Geoff had been in the artillery until 1942 when he joined the RAAF (Royal Australian Air Force). The following year he was posted to Britain, just in time for the assault on Berlin. Ken was glad that the Aussie was 'Tail-End Charlie', the main defence of the 'Lanc'. Geoff was one of the best – cool, calm and alert. He had survived over 20 missions and already had one night fighter to his credit, a Junkers 88 shot down on 2 December.

Pilot – Flight Sergeant Ken Doyle
Rear gunner – Flight Sergeant Geoffrey C. C. Smith
Upper turret gunner – Sergeant Nobby Clarke
Wireless operator – Sergeant Don Green
Navigator – Sergeant Winlow
Flight engineer – Sergeant Syd Richardson
Bomb aimer – Sergeant Alf Astle

The crew of Lancaster ND444 GT-O in order of appearance in this chapter.

Ken was right, experience counted. Thirty miles from Berlin Geoff snapped out a warning over the intercom, 'Fighter coming in.' He had spotted an Me 110 dead astern and 650 m below. Yet spotted was hardly the word. The fighter's red and green navigation lights flicked on and off. The German might as well have carried a neon sign flashing 'Here I am'. It was too easy. He was either a fool, suicidal or . . .

'There's two of them,' Geoff yelled. 'I'll watch this one. Look out for the other Jerry, Nobby.'

Nobby Clarke was upper turret gunner. He had

Tail-End Charlie on a 'Lanc' in his Fraser-Nash rear gun turret.

barely time to scan the darkness before all hell let loose.

'Skipper. Corkscrew Port! Go! Go! Go!' the Australian commanded. The 110 had suddenly closed in – firing! Ken obeyed at once. In an attack from behind the rear gunner gave the orders. (Corkscrewing was a violent emergency manoeuvre to lose attacking fighters. The plane flipped sharply to one side and dived almost vertically before levelling out again.) As the Lancaster banked Geoff opened up. His four machine-guns tore into the fighter and abruptly it blew apart, the explosion illuminating the sky. But at almost the same moment glowing strings of green tracer whipped past Geoff's turret and he felt a stunning wave of pain surging from his right ankle. The other Jerry had made his move.

Geoff's order to corkscrew hadn't come a second too soon. A Focke-Wulf had pounced, pumping a hail of cannon shells along the length of the Lancaster's fuselage. As the second fighter disappeared into the night the RAF bomber was left stricken. The hydraulic lines were cut and the escaping hydraulic oil burst into flames. Left without power both turrets and the bomb doors were almost useless. Nobby's left leg was broken by a cannon shell and riddled with steel splinters. As he fell the oxygen line was ripped from his face-mask and he passed out. Geoff was writhing in agony – he had been hit by a cannon shell that had almost severed his foot.

Heading Home

The fighter attack and the bomber's escape were over in seconds, but they were seconds that changed the mission. As soon as Ken levelled out he began to assess the damage. Anxiously he called each crewman on the intercom. There was no reply from Nobby, and he could hear Geoff groaning in the rear turret. The first decision was the hardest. With the bomb doors jammed it was clear that pushing on to Berlin was pointless. Only 15 miles from the target Ken turned reluctantly for England. Now it was time to patch up the crew and the almost defenceless aircraft.

The wireless operator, Sergeant Don Green, went back to help Nobby, who was gasping for air. Don slipped a spare oxygen lead into the gunner's mouth, made him comfortable and took his place. The navigator, Sergeant Winlow, went to investigate the fire and rescue Geoff. With relief, he found the only thing still burning was the Australian's parachute. Using an extinguisher he put out the blaze and then tried to persuade Geoff to leave his precious guns. Incredibly, although he was losing a lot of blood, the stubborn Aussie refused. Geoff knew there was still a high risk of another fighter attack. In spite of the pain and the lack of power he could still operate his turret by hand. While they were over enemy territory he insisted he was going to stay put.

Luckily the crew of ND444 avoided the further unwelcome attentions of the Luftwaffe but their troubles were far from over. As they neared the coast they came under intense fire from anti-aircraft guns. Flak burst around the Lanc and two engines were hit. Ken promptly shut them down, but now they were limping home. If either of the surviving Merlins played up they would be ditching in the freezing North Sea.

The next snag was to dump the bombs. The last thing they wanted was an emergency landing with a full bomb load. A crash or a fire and . . . BOOM! Sergeant Syd Richardson, the flight engineer, crawled into the bomb bay inspection hatch and dismantled the connections to the wrecked hydraulic system. In theory, when they jettisoned the bombs, their weight should force open the bomb doors. The theory worked — almost. The deadly load fell away cleanly into the sea, except for one jammed 500 lb (220 kg) bomb. Syd had done wonders but the landing had better be smooth.

Once over the coast it was also time to prise Geoff out of his turret. And it wasn't going to be easy. The flip doors into the gun turret had frozen solid and the only thing to do was chop through them with a fire axe. For over half an hour bomb aimer Sergeant Alf Astle, helped by Don Green, hacked at the doors until they had made a gap big enough to drag Geoff through. They were horrified when they peered inside. His smashed leg was entangled in the ammunition belts and the turret seemed to have been sprayed with blood. When they pulled him out they gave Geoff a shot of **morphine** to ease the pain and he slipped into a merciful sleep. Now all they needed was a safe landing, but the odds did not look good.

Ken radioed ahead for permission to land at the emergency runway at Woodbridge on the Suffolk coast. As they approached his thoughts raced through the problems facing him. The undercarriage had been shot up. Although it had lowered, would it collapse when he touched down? Then there were the bomb doors. Still open, they dragged like an enormous brake. The trim of the plane had gone to pot. And best not to even think about the bomb still aboard.

Grimly, Ken alerted the airfield that they better give

him plenty of room for a belly landing. Finally he warned the crew they were going in and asked them to do what they could to protect the injured gunners. Tenderly, they packed themselves around Nobby and Geoff and braced for impact.

At 1:50 the Lancaster touched down, the engines revving hard to avoid stalling. The starboard tyre burst and the plane slewed a little but the undercarriage held. To Ken's amazement they were down in one piece.

At once the crew sprang into action. They chopped a large hole in the fuselage and lifted the wounded men into a waiting ambulance. Geoff was rushed to Ely hospital but his leg was too badly damaged to save – it was amputated above the knee. The stubborn gunner was awarded a CGM (Conspicuous Gallantry Medal) for staying at his post to protect his Lancaster and crew. As usual his reaction was modest. 'If it hadn't been for the skipper, we'd never have got back at all.'

In 1945 Geoff Smith returned to Australia and became a successful businessman. He didn't let his lack of a leg get him down, always believing, 'I'm as good as the next guy.' But sadly this story doesn't have a happy ending for everyone. In war, fate is never fair and one brush with danger doesn't guarantee safety in the future. Ken Doyle, Alf Astle and Don Green were killed in September 1944 on a mission over Calais. Their plane was hit by flak and crashed in the sea. Their bodies were never found.

FIGHTING FACTS

The Cost

Of the 891 bombers that took off on Geoff Smith's raid, 42 were shot down and two crashed in England. That was almost 5 per cent of the total force – light losses. During the next raid on Berlin, on 21 March, 72 planes were lost out of 809, almost 9 per cent. Throughout the war 56,000 aircrew of RAF Bomber Command were killed. Of these, 40 per cent came from the Commonwealth and other countries that rallied to the Allied cause.

Turret Terrors

The rear turret of the bomber was the most dangerous place on the plane. Most Luftwaffe pilots preferred to attack from behind and slightly below. If they killed the rear gunner in their first burst the bomber was helpless. Worse, the German night fighters had better weapons. Their 20 mm or 30 mm cannon had more firing power and a longer range than the dated British machine-guns.

Top Tips for Rear Turret Gunners

Gunners learned by experience and passed tips on to one another. Good advice from old hands saved the lives of new recruits:

- Remember the rear turret is the coldest place on the plane, sometimes down to – 40 degrees at 15,000 feet (4,500 m). Watch out for frostbite. Wear as much clothing as possible – silk underwear, woollen pullovers, extra woollen socks, electrically heated suit. You'll feel like the **Michelin Man** but every layer is vital.

- Cover all your exposed flesh in lanolin and wear elastoplast on your cheeks to stop the metal studs on your flying helmet from freezing to your skin.

- Wear sunglasses for half an hour before take-off to get your eyes used to night vision.

- Always carry a 'panic bowler', a steel helmet – not for your head, stupid! Put it in your seat cushion to protect your most important bits.

- Make sure the perspex canopy is spotlessly clean. Watch out for old perspex, it scratches easily and can be difficult to see through. Best take out the rear-centre panel. OK, it's a lot colder, if that seems possible, but you get a clear view. It's your choice, freeze or die.

- Shave before take-off. Stubble can be irritating inside a rubber face oxygen mask. And don't forget to squeeze the oxygen tube regularly during the flight. If ice crystals form and block the tube you might pass out. If no one revives you quickly, that's it, mate.

- Remember good luck charms and rituals before take-off – a little of your girlfriend's perfume, a love letter, a rabbit's foot, a Cornish pixie, a silver three-penny bit. Yeah, it's stupid, but you never know …

- If a night fighter attacks – wait, wait, WAIT! His cannon have a longer range, but he needs to get close to be sure of a kill. Let him come in to 500 yards or less if you've got the nerve. Then let him have it.

Main Bomber Command aircraft in the Battle of Britain

Type	Max. Speed	Range	Weapons	Comment
Avro Lancaster	281 mph (450 kph) at 11,000 ft (3,353 m) with extra fuel and 7,000 lb (3,175 kg) bomb load	1,040 miles (1,670 km) or 2,680 miles (4,310 km)	14,000 lb (6,350 kg) bomb load. Eight .303 machine-guns.	A large stable plane that could take a lot of punishment. The backbone of Bomber Command from 1943.
Mosquito	408 mph (655 kph) at 26,000 ft (9,048 m)	1,370 miles (2,200 km)	4,000 lb (1,800 kg)	A fast, light bomber, built from plywood. No guns were fitted in the bomber version, because it could out-run most fighters.
Handley-Page Halifax Mk I	265 mph (426 kph)	1,860 miles (2990 km) at 17,500 ft (5,334m) with 5,800 lb bomb load	5,800 lb (2,635 kg) bomb load. Eight .303 machine-guns.	The first true heavy bomber produced in large numbers for the RAF.

One City Too Far

The plan to bomb Germany into submission was controversial during World War II and has been argued about ever since. But the destruction of one city above all others has come to symbolize the cruelty of war – Dresden.

Dresden was the capital of Saxony, in southern Germany. It was an ancient town with many wooden buildings and a maze of narrow streets in the centre. By early 1945 it was packed with refugees and troops running away from Russian armies. Although it had no major industries, Bomber Command was running out of new targets and Dresden came up on the hit list. On the night of 13/14 February 805 aircraft attacking in two waves dropped 2,659 tons of high explosive and incendiary (fire) bombs. During daylight on 14 and 15 February the Americans blitzed the city again with 600 more bombers. The results were horrendous. A fire-storm swept Dresden and 35,000 people died.

Repairing the Scars of War

One British bomber pilot, 31-year-old Flight Lieutenant Frank Smith of 57 Squadron, looked down from his plane at the blazing city and shuddered. He was haunted by his part in the raids on Dresden for the rest of his life. His son Alan remembers: 'In his eyes it was nothing to boast about. He tried to instil in us all as children the horror of it all.'

Frank died in 1982, but eighteen years later in a strange twist of fate, Alan Smith found himself helping to repair the scars of war. On 14 February 2000, the 55th anniversary of the raids, he presented Dresden with an 8m-high golden cross and orb. This will sit atop the city's most famous church, the Frauenkirche. This medieval

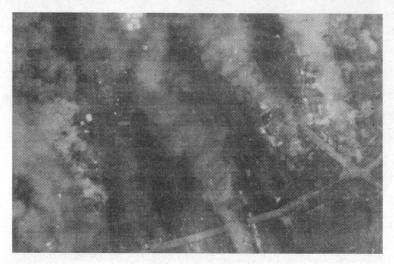

The ruins of Dresden.

masterpiece was destroyed in 1945 and is still being rebuilt. The massive project will last until 2006.

Alan worked for a London firm of silversmiths and was delighted when they won the contract to make the new cross. This cost £300,000, and in an act of reconciliation the money was raised in Britain. When the 1.25-ton cross was finished, his boss couldn't think of anyone more fitting than a bomber pilot's son to present it. After the solemn handover Alan commented, 'My father would have been filled with pride. My family and I want to say sorry for what happened.'

THE YANKS ARE COMING

BATTLE BRIEFING

Eighth Air Force

In December 1941 the United States was dragged into World War II by the shock Japanese attack on Pearl Harbor. In spite of this, the Americans agreed that the greatest danger came from Germany and that Hitler should be defeated first. Like the British, they believed that the war could be won by the relentless use of bombers.

In February 1942 Major-General Carl Spaatz arrived in Britain to set up the European wing of the United States Army Air Force – the Eighth Air Force. Within a year over 100 new airfields had been built across East Anglia and 'round the clock bombing' of Germany was under way – the Americans by day and the British by night. 'Snuffy' Smith was one of the army of American 'flyboys' posted to England in 1943.

'SNUFFY' SMITH

Ball Turret Gunner

No one could remember how Sergeant 'Snuffy' Smith got his nickname. In fact, before 1 May 1943 there wasn't anything much to remember about Snuffy at all. His real name was Maynard Harrison Smith. He was small, slim and neat – a tax clerk from Carol, Michigan, where he lived with his parents on South State Street.

Snuffy enlisted in the United States Army Air Force in 1942 and trained as a crewman for bombers. His size meant he was selected as a gunner for the ball turret of a Boeing B-17 Fortress – a cramped, perspex and metal globe hung under the fuselage of the plane. He was 32, an 'old man' amongst thousands of 18 and 19-year-old recruits. Perhaps a little too old, because he didn't suffer Air Force discipline easily and earned a reputation as an awkward character.

In the spring of 1943 Snuffy was sent to England and assigned to the 423rd Bombardment Squadron – a unit of the 'Mighty' Eighth Air Force in England. The British bombed Germany under protection of darkness but the Americans were convinced they could hit the enemy harder with daylight raids. So from August 1942 ever-larger formations of heavily armed bombers probed into France and then Germany itself. The cost was high.

B-17 bombers carried a crew of ten and bristled

A B-17 in flight.

with machine-guns. To give mutual protection they flew in tight box formations of eighteen aircraft and could lay down awesome firepower if jumped from astern or abeam. Yet they were easy meat for Nazi fighters, especially the fearsome Focke-Wulf Fw 190s. German pilots soon learned that a head on attack – a sharp burst of cannon shells into the cockpit – meant a quick end to a bomber. Snuffy and the other new recruits were all too often filling the gaps caused by mounting losses.

First Mission

On 1 May the 423rd Bombardment Squadron was ordered to join 60 other B-17s in an attack on the French port of St Nazaire, a base for U-boats – German submarines. 1st Lieutenant Lewis Page Johnson, skipper of Fortress 42-29649, hoped for an easy ride. It was his last combat flight before his tour of duty, 25 missions, was complete. The USA beckoned.

Many American bombers were boldly decorated – with names like Pistol Packin' Mama or Yankee Doodle. Johnson would have none of this. He didn't want anything on his plane that might make a Jerry fighter look twice. It was to this careful pilot that Snuffy was assigned for his first mission.

The raid ran like clockwork. No fighters and only light

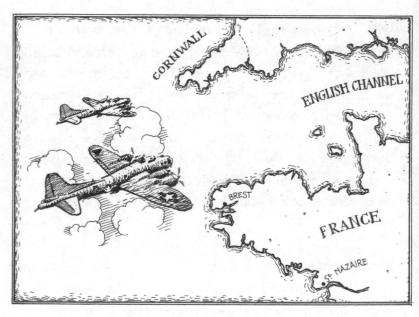

The attack on St Nazaire.

flak (anti-aircraft fire). The gleaming bombers reached their target, released their bombs and turned for home. They were over water and could see land ahead. Surely this meant England and safety! Johnson even joked that they'd have to ditch in the sea so he'd have a good story to tell his kids. In the history of mistimed wit, this quip was a whammy. Suddenly, all hell let loose.

Unknowingly, the B-17s had left St Nazaire in the wrong direction and flown towards the Brest Peninsula. They were still over France! As the Fortress crossed the coastline a hail of flak burst around the formation. Co-pilot Bob McCallum recalled:

> We had stumbled into a French port – navigator's error ... First one of our wingmen went down and then the other. We pulled into a tight turn and got out of there. We took a heading due north and stepped on the gas. And then the fighters ripped in at about 3 o'clock (above right) through the haze. We broke away, went right down on the deck and hedge hopped to shake the Jerries off. It worked.

Or so Bob thought. They turned north for England and he had just begun to breathe again when more Fw 190 fighters attacked. 20 mm cannon fire tore through the thin aluminium fuselage and to his dismay 'the whole ship shook and kind of bonged, like a sound effect in a Disney movie'. In seconds the Fortress was ablaze with many of the controls shot out. Captain Ray J. Check, flying another plane close by, later reported: 'Except for the nose and cockpit, flames completely filled the ship . . . it was like a comet.'

The first Snuffy knew of the threat was enemy tracer shells whipping past his turret. Moments later he was shaken by a huge explosion. Urgently, he tried the intercom to the Skipper – nothing. Next he tried to rotate the turret to climb out – nothing. The power was down. Slowly he hand-cranked himself into the fuselage and climbed out to see two fires raging, a fierce one in the radio compartment and a second smaller blaze in the tail section.

As the stunned gunner tried to take in what was happening, the radio operator staggered out of his tiny compartment and dived out of the gun hatch. Snuffy knew he was jumping to almost certain death: 'Even though his chute opened, the poor guy's Mae West (life jacket) had been burned off and we were over plenty of water.'

Yet the horror of burning to death was so great that the port waist gunner had also tried to bale out but hadn't quite made it. He was trapped, half in and half out of the Fortress – his parachute harness snagged on his gun mounting.

'Hey, buddy, is it too hot for you?' Snuffy quipped as he pulled him back aboard.

The waist gunner stared at him as if he was mad and snapped, 'I'm getting out of here.'

There was no point in arguing. Snuffy helped him open

the rear escape hatch and watched as he jumped clear. He wished the crewman luck but had no time to waste, the smoke and gas in the plane were building up fast.

Firefighter

Despite the damage, the Fortress was flying level and Snuffy guessed the skipper must still be at the controls. With that hope in his mind, he decided to stay and fight the fires. Wrapping a sweater round his face to shield his eyes and throat, he grabbed an extinguisher and began to tackle the blaze in the radio compartment. At first the flames flared up but then slowly began to die away. Snuffy was just making headway when he glanced round to check the tail section – and saw movement. He recalled:

> I found the tail gunner painfully crawling back from his turret. I saw he had been hit in the back. I guessed a shell had gone through his left lung, so I laid him down on his left side to keep the blood from draining into his right lung and slowly drowning him. I gave him a shot of morphine and made him as comfortable as possible.

No sooner had Snuffy picked up the extinguisher again than another, more deadly, interruption appeared. He saw an Fw 190 zooming in from the side. With amazing cool, he gave it a burst from the right-waist gun and stepped across the plane to fire a second blast from the left-waist gun as the fighter swept underneath.

The next frantic minutes saw Snuffy leaping between tasks – fireman, gunner and paramedic. Using the remaining extinguishers he dowsed the forward blaze, spraying the last bottle over the smouldering control cables. The fuselage around the radio compartment was so badly damaged that large holes had been burned through the skin of the Fortress. Using these to his advantage he hurled smouldering wreckage and red-hot ammunition cans overboard.

Persistently, an Fw 190 pumped cannon shells into the stricken Fortress. Whether it was the same fighter, or newcomers joining in the kill, Snuffy couldn't tell. Each time he broke off and grabbed the nearest gun to return fire. Nervously he kept a couple of the hot ammunition cans to hand, ready to fend off any more visits by the Focke-Wulfs, but fearful in case they blew up.

Now Snuffy made a fateful decision. To move faster he took his parachute off and tied his fate to that of the plane and his wounded companion. With the Fortress flying at low altitude he wouldn't have time to put it on again before they crashed. Still, it was as well he hadn't removed it earlier. As he eased the pack off his aching back he saw it had stopped a bullet, probably from an exploding ammo can.

Turning to the smaller fire in the tail Snuffy faced a dangerous problem. The extinguishers were empty. Scrambling through the debris he found a water bottle and emptied it over the hottest part. After this there was nothing else to do but to try to smother the blaze with his hands and feet. Padding and stamping like a wild dancer he slowly snuffed it out – but not before his clothes had begun to smoulder.

Rough Landing

With the fire finally out Snuffy looked through a hatchway and caught his breath. He could see a coastline ahead and prayed that it was England. He knelt down and told the wounded tail gunner that safety was near but his own thoughts were not so confident. If they managed to locate an airfield would the battered plane survive a rough landing? Snuffy remembers:

I could tell she was acting tail heavy so I tossed overboard everything I could break loose – guns, ammunition, clothes, everything. I knew the tail wheel was gone and I was afraid the shock of the landing would break the 'Fort' in half.

In the cockpit Johnson had the same doubts. Bailing out seemed a good idea but he had two wounded crewmen in the nose section. Another option was ditching in the sea, but he was fairly sure the fire would have destroyed the dinghies. Like Snuffy he concluded he was there for the full ride.

After such a grim flight, any crew deserved a little good luck and Johnson sighed with relief when he saw an airfield ahead. It was Predannack in Cornwall. At least the navigation was correct this time. Now for the landing. Sweating with tension he brought the shattered Fortress in as easily as he could with the few remaining controls. With an ominous rumble she hit the runway – but held together. They were down.

When the wounded had been rushed to hospital, Johnson and Snuffy surveyed the damage:

- radio compartment and tail section burnt out;
- mid fuselage torn apart by cannon shells and internal fire;
- oxygen system ruptured – adding to the intensity of the fire;
- top turret disabled by cannon fire;
- tail wheel gear damaged;
- nose section shattered by cannon fire;
- petrol tank in port wing burnt out;
- No. 4 engine **nacelle** shot off.

It was quite a list. Johnson wouldn't have to make up any stories for his kids after all.

Difficult Hero

In his mission report Johnson gave fulsome praise to his turret gunner. He wrote: '... his acts performed in complete self-sacrifice were solely responsible for the safe return of the aeroplane, the life of the tail gunner and the lives of everyone else aboard.' As a result Snuffy was awarded the Congressional Medal of Honour, only the second Eighth Air Force serviceman to win this rare honour.

Snuffy flew four more combat missions but he remained 'difficult to handle'. Only four days before the award ceremony, he was on punishment duty in the station mess hall. Imagine the embarrassment for the USAAF! The press loved the Snuffy story and he had become an all-American hero. But senior officers in the 423rd were almost relieved when he was withdrawn from service and sent home. Ironically, he was now far more useful touring the USA to rally the fighting spirit of the American public.

Old heroes are often forgotten, but not Snuffy. When he died in 1984 he was buried in Arlington National Cemetery with full military honours.

FIGHTING FACTS

Daylight Bombing

Heavy losses had convinced the RAF that night bombing was the only way to reduce casualties. In 1942, however, the Eighth Air Force arrived in Britain sure they had the planes and technology to bomb in daylight. These included:

- The Boeing B-17 heavy bomber, bristling with machine-guns and flying in box formations to give mutual covering fire.

- Self-regulating oxygen systems for the crew, and a turbo-supercharger for the engines, so that planes could fly at high altitudes – 25,000 feet and more.
- The Norden bombsight – an electro-mechanical computer that could 'drop a bomb into a pickle-barrel from 20,000 ft (6,095 m)'.

American Planes in the Daylight Battle Over Europe

Type	Max. Speed	Range	Weapons	Comment
Boeing B-17F Flying Fortress	299 mph (480 kph)	17,000 miles (27,350 km) at 30,000 ft (9,140 m) with Tokyo tanks (extra fuel tanks in the wings)	Up to thirteen .50 inch Browning machine-guns.	The 'Fort' could take heavy damage and was liked by crews.
North American P-51 Mustang	437 mph (705 kph) at 25,000 ft (7,620 m)	2,080 miles (3,345 km) with drop tanks	Six .05 calibre machine-guns.	The best Allied escort fighter of World War II.

Daylight Disappointment

The Eighth Air Force was in for a shock. German defences were far better than expected and the technology did not always work.

German fighters were armed with 20 mm or 30 mm cannon that could rip the aluminium structure of the B-17s apart.

Heavy 105 mm flak guns could hurl time-fused shells to a height of 31,000 feet (9,445 m), high enough to hit any Allied bomber.

The Norden bombsight had worked well on tests in sunny California, but in cloudy, rain-soaked European skies it was disappointing.

One in Three

In 1943–44 American losses were high. Two of the worst raids were on the small industrial town of Schweinfurt to knock out ball-bearing factories:

14 August 1943

Number of planes on mission	320
Number of planes shot down	60

17 August 1943

Number of planes on mission	230
Number of planes shot down	36

The Germans only lost 25 fighters.

A standard tour of duty for members of a bomber crew was 25 missions. That earned a ticket home! But with odds like those in the table, it was no wonder that aircrew believed they only had a one in three chance of surviving the tour.

Little Friends

It was soon clear that the bombers could not be expected to protect themselves against Nazi fighters. Escorts were needed. P-47 Thunderbolts and P-38 Lightnings were used at first but they barely had the range to reach the German border. In December 1943 however, the answer roared in – the P-51 Mustang. Fitted with the Rolls Royce Merlin engine and drop tanks it became a war winner. By early 1944 the bomber crews, guarded by what they called their 'Little Friends', stood a far better chance of survival.

Combat Witness

I can say with truth I'd rather face a fighter than flak. A fighter you can do something about, but flak you can't.
John Butler of the 93rd Bombardment Group

The bombers had to stay on course – and once they were on their bomb-run, which was where the German fighters hit them, they couldn't deviate at all. They just had to plough on and when they were hit, they just blew right up, their whole bomb load went right up, and where an aeroplane had been there was just a smoke ring.
Lt-Colonel Jim Goodson of the 4th Fighter Group

His gun was frozen and he sat helplessly watching repeated fighter attacks ... the No.2 engine was hit and caught fire ... a plane on his wing went out of control ... and crashed into a bomber on their opposite side. The pilot had to take evasive action to miss pieces

of B-17 that were flying in the air. He saw the ball
turret knocked off and go down like an apple with the
gunner still inside. He saw another man jump with a
burning parachute and go down like a lump of lead.
Medical report on an exhausted gunner after a raid
on Kiel, 13 June 1943

Nose Art

Unlike Lieutenant Johnson, most American captains liked
a lively name and a vivid image painted on the nose of
their bombers. Some were given daring names:

KNOCK-OUT DROPPER
DEE-FEATER
HELLSADROPPIN
BOMB BOOGIE

Others were called after cartoon characters:

SNOW WHITE
MICKEY MOUSE
BUGS BUNNY
POPEYE

But pin-up girls were by far the most popular. The ruder
the better:

DINAH MIGHT
ICE COLD KATE
IZA VAILABLE
SLICK CHICK
HUSSLIN' HUSSY

East Anglia – USA

England was invaded during World War II – by friendly 'Yanks'. By June 1944 there were 300,000 Eighth Air Force personnel alone, most of them in East Anglia. Dozens of new airfields had to be built, each like a small town. A typical base needed a concrete runway a mile in length, two smaller back-up runways, hardstanding for the planes, 30 miles of drains, 500 separate buildings and a sewerage plant for 2,500 people. Most of these airfields were built by Irish navies or black GIs. (GI = General Infantryman or ordinary soldier.)

Memories of Britain

Rain

Most Americans hated the rain and dismal overcast skies. The 384th Bomb Group, based at Grafton Underwood in Northamptonshire, soon renamed their airfield Grafton Undermud.

Stinky Brits

A common view was that British bathrooms were primitive and underused. Some Yanks called England 'Goatland'.

Love

But the smell can't have been that bad. Love bloomed during the war. Around 35,000 British women married Americans and returned to the USA with them.

American servicemen were issued with guides on how to behave in Britain. Advice included:

- 'stop and think before you sound off about the lukewarm beer'
- 'don't show off or brag or bluster'
- 'don't make wisecracks about British defeats'
- 'don't make fun of British speech' and, most important of all,
- 'NEVER criticize the King or Queen.'

Rationing Riches

By 1943 rationing was biting hard in Britain, especially for children. Ice cream manufacture was banned from September 1942 until March 1945 and sweets were in short supply. In contrast the Americans seemed like rich relations. US servicemen were much better paid than the British and they had PX stores (military shops with goods shipped in from America) full of endless supplies of chocolates and chewing gum.

Americans were always surrounded by kids yelling, 'Got any gum, chum?'

To which the fast reply was, 'Gotta sister, mister?'

Spotting a chance for good public relations, the USAF laid on 379 parties for over 50,000 British children between July 1942 and July 1944.

OPERATION JERICHO

BATTLE BRIEFING

Resistance

In 1940 France fell to Nazi invaders after only six weeks of fighting. For some French people this was too much to bear and Resistance groups sprang up all over the country. Operating undercover, these freedom fighters hit back against the German army of occupation. They rescued shot-down aircrew and helped them escape to Britain, spied for the Allies, supplying information about German forces, and even sabotaged troop trains. If caught, they faced imprisonment in concentration camps or execution.

Invasion Threatened

By late 1943 there was a terrible crisis. The Allies were planning to invade, landing on the Normandy coast. The British and Americans needed the eyes, ears and fighting spirit of the Resistance more than ever. The Germans knew an invasion was coming and were equally determined to stamp out any secret armies behind their lines. They set up a force of collaborators, other French people prepared to seek out and betray those fighting for freedom. By the winter of 1943–44 this plan was so successful that a member of the Resistance was lucky to survive six months without being arrested and shot. The lingering bitterness caused by collaboration still troubles France today.

The Allies were particularly worried about the situation in northern France around the town of Amiens. They needed all

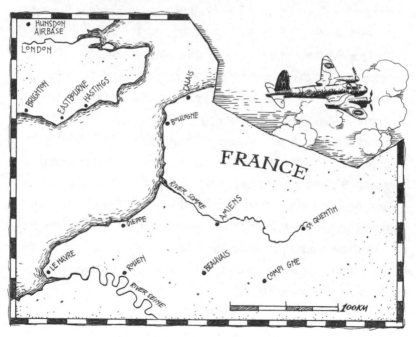

The town of Amiens in northern France.

the information they could get on the menacing V1 flying bomb sites (see chapter 6). If these missiles were fired in large numbers at Britain, then the invasion itself might be held up – or even abandoned. Yet so many people had been arrested that the Resistance network was on the point of collapse. Among them were key fighters such as the young and brave Jean Beaurin. Jean had led daring raids against the railways and blown up five troop trains, killing and injuring thousands of Germans and destroying their tanks and vehicles. At the beginning of 1944 the grim cells of Amiens prison were packed with 700 prisoners who, if tortured, might give away others. And worse, on 19 February, over a hundred were to be executed.

The Resistance had one unbreakable rule: if comrades were caught, the others had to try to save them. But, already weakened, how could they break into a heavily guarded prison and rescue so many? Their leader, Dominique Ponchardier, turned to Britain for help. Plans of the prison, the defences and the duty rosters of the guards were gathered at great risk and sent to London. Dominique also sent a daunting message. Could the RAF burst open Amiens prison and free the prisoners? Once they were out, Resistance teams would be waiting to hide them. If not, could the bombers destroy the prison? It was better for captured comrades to die than give away others.

PRISON BUSTERS

Basil Embry's Dilemma

The Amiens problem was dropped in the lap of Air Vice Marshall Basil Embry, a pint-sized ball of energy who made bigger men quake. Basil was Commander of 2 Group – twelve squadrons equipped with Mosquitoes, the fastest fighter-bombers flown by the Allies. Among his exploits was a daring escape from France in 1940. Captured after his plane was shot down, Basil killed his guards and crossed the Pyrenees to Spain – with the help of a Resistance group. He owed the French a personal favour.

Yet even Basil was dismayed by this mission. It would be easy enough to blast the prison to rubble, he thought, but to damage it just enough to allow a mass break-out? Now that was a tall order. Calling together his planning group, he shared his dilemma: 'We know, and so do those who have asked us to try and do this, that no matter how precise the bombing, many prisoners are liable to be killed too. I'm assured they accept this fact and therefore so must we.'

Like Joshua in the Bible, 2 Group had to bring the walls of Amiens prison tumbling down. It was little wonder then that the mission was named 'Operation Jericho'. With barely a month to go, the 'backroom boys' worked out every painstaking detail at breakneck speed. If they got it wrong, the Resistance fighters would pay with their lives.

Operation Jericho

The Target

Amiens prison was built on the outskirts of the town, next to the main road from Albert. It was a cross-shaped three-storey building, surrounded by a 20 ft (6 m) high perimeter wall. The prisoners were held in the longer arm of the cross, with the guards housed in extensions at each end. If the weather was clear, the Route d'Albert pointed to the target like a giant arrow. To focus thinking, a scale model gave a pilot's eye view of the prison from four miles away. This was made by 2 Group model shop, using aerial photographs and plans supplied by the Resistance. It became the centre of intense briefings as tactics were thrashed out.

Model of Amiens prison used to brief the Mosquito crews.

The raid was set to go any day from 10 February onwards – on the first fine day. But their time of arrival was crucial. It had to be noon. At midday the guards gathered in their mess hall for lunch – sitting targets! Wipe them out and the whole escape became much simpler. The streets too would be quiet, lessening the chance of killing innocent civilians.

The Leader

Group Captain Percy Pickard was to lead the attack. Better known as 'Pick' to his aircrews, he was a reluctant hero, a gentle giant who never wanted to kill anyone. But he had soon proved that he was good – very good at war. Like Basil, he too owed a debt to the French. On 24 February 1943 he had made a secret landing in a remote area. He had flown in at night to drop agents and supplies for the Resistance. His plane bogged down and almost everyone in the local village, including the police, worked furiously to pull the aircraft free. As he took off the Gestapo were already closing in. Tragically, some of those who helped him were caught.

The Men and the Machines

Mosquito fighter-bombers, 'Mossies', were the best planes for low-level, precision bombing. And this was a roof-top attack – the planes had to zoom in at 240 mph (385 kph), only 10 feet (3 m) above the ground. If the pilots released their bombs too soon, too high or too fast, there was a good chance they would bounce right over the target.

Basil picked the three squadrons of 140 Wing, based at Hunsdon, near London, for the Amiens mission. They were amongst his most experienced pilots and had spent the winter blitzing flying bomb sites. Eighteen planes, six from each squadron, would attack in three waves.

No. 487 Squadron, New Zealanders, had two objectives:

- Blast holes in the east and north sides of the perimeter wall. If only one side was breached the guards might be able to seal the gap with vehicles or machine-guns.
- Score a direct hit on the mess hall to kill and injure as many guards as possible. With luck, the survivors would be too confused to stop the breakout.

No. 464 Squadron, Australians, had the most delicate task of all:

- Blow the main building to make holes large enough for the prisoners to escape. The shock from the explosions should also shake open the cell doors.

No. 21 Squadron, British, drew the short straw. They had to stand off and watch the attack. If the raid failed to crack open the prison, 'Pick' would call them in to destroy it!

By the morning of Friday, 18 February even the steel nerves of Basil Embry were beginning to fray. For over a week the weather had been atrocious across Europe. Blizzards had swept the airfield and snow blanketed the ground. Even a kite would have had trouble getting aloft. But time had run out. The prisoners would be shot tomorrow. It was now or never.

The crews were called in for briefing and the final call, left to Group Captain Pickard. Pick studied the latest forecast. There would be no improvement over Britain, but there was a chance of clear skies over France. With two hours to the deadline he made the decision to go.

Two hours – a lifetime of waiting for the airmen. Jericho was tricky. It was almost certain there would be casualties. To ease tension the banter flew thick and fast:

'If you stare at those pin-ups any longer, you'll go blind.'

'Don't forget your life jacket – it helps the rescue teams find your body.'

Breakfast helped – an endless supply of fried eggs, strictly rationed for civilians. After that a brief time to relax – billiards, the Glenn Miller orchestra on the radio, reading, letter-writing to girlfriends or wives – just in case! Soon the mess was a fug of tobacco smoke.

Outside, the ground crews were in a flurry of activity. Engineers and electricians tested and retested systems; engines were run up and exhaust smoke drifted across

Group Captain Percy Pickard (left) and Flight Lieutenant Bill Broadly (right)
get ready for take-off on the Amiens raid.

the airfield; trolley drivers trundled out the 500 lb (225 kg) bombs; armourers prepared the ammunition belts, feeding them carefully into their narrow boxes. And still the unforgiving snow pelted down.

By 10:30 everyone was at dispersal, waiting for the final word. Surely in this weather it was impossible? Then Pick roared up, wound down the window of his car and yelled, 'Time, gentlemen, please.' Shuffling out in their thick flying boots the crews piled into trucks for the short run to the 'Mossies'. Once aboard the exhaustive cockpit drill began:

'Check petrol-cocks.'

'Petrol-cocks SET.'

'Check booster-pumps.'

'Booster-pumps ON.'

Like priest and congregation, pilot and navigator said their responses, as if reciting a fervent prayer. And in a way they were. This was their final, life-saving inspection of the plane. From engines to oxygen, if there was a fault, please let it show now.

Visibility Nil

With Merlins roaring, the Mosquitoes taxied to the downwind side of the airfield and lined up in pairs. At intervals of 100 yards (90 m) they took off from east to west. Throttles open, the aircraft tore down the runway, hugging the ground until they reached safety speed, 170 mph. By a little after 11:00 the last of the raiders was airborne. But the Mossies were climbing into the worst conditions the crews had ever known.

At 100 feet (30 m) above the runway visibility was nil. Dick Sugden of 464 Squadron recalled: 'We never saw anyone else. It was like flying in a blancmange.' Blind, the navigators used compass, map and ground radar to head for Littlehampton and the rendezvous with an escort of Typhoon fighters. Soon, four aircraft had lost their way, crews straining to see through snow-spattered canopies. As the minutes ticked by, they realized bitterly that they would arrive too late. Since timing was vital, one by one they turned for home. Not yet over France and a quarter of the strike force was gone!

As Dick Sugden neared Littlehampton (he hoped) the cloud suddenly cleared. There was the sea ahead of them, gleaming in the sun. And there was another Mossie breaking cloud and swerving right in front of them!

Dick heaved on the control column and almost cartwheeled his plane to avoid a smash. The plane juddered fiercely and seemed ready to tear apart.

'Get out of it, you idiot,' he yelled over the radio.

As the other plane wheeled urgently away Dick glimpsed its Id letter. 'God,' he thought, 'It's "F" for Freddy – Pick's plane'. Gulping he remembered the CO's last words at the briefing: 'I want complete radio silence. If any fool opens his mouth up there he'll be off my station tonight.'

Not only had Dick disobeyed, he had done so to curse Pick himself. But at least they hadn't collided!

They're Here

In Amiens prison Jean Beaurin stood at the small window of his cell. News of the RAF raid had been smuggled into the jail and each day since he had anxiously scanned the sky. In the distance a church bell dolefully tolled noon as if marking a funeral – his own. Yet as the bell faded, air raid sirens ripped the air. In the distance he could hear the throb of aircraft engines. 'Get down,' he yelled to his cellmates. 'They're here.'

It had been a spectacular trip. The Mosquitoes had skimmed over the channel at over 300 mph, their propeller tips barely 15 feet above the sea. They had hoped to duck under the German radar, but the powerful Wurzburg sets had detected them. Soon the run to Amiens became a series of doglegs designed to fool enemy fighter controllers and side-step anti-aircraft batteries. Ten minutes from the target, Q for Queenie, flown by 'Tich' Hanafin, was caught by flak. He turned for home badly wounded, the Mossie limping on one engine. Meanwhile, only a few kilometres from the target, the 'Abbeville Boys', the toughest Luftwaffe unit in France, were ordered to stand by for immediate take-off.

At 12:03 the first wave of Mosquitoes from 487 Squadron swept in along the Route d'Albert. They were so low that section leader 'Black' Smith had to watch his wings didn't clip the telegraph poles. Suddenly the prison appeared, standing out like a grey castle in the bleak winter landscape. 'It looks just like the briefing model,' yelled Pilot Officer Sparkes.

The last minute passed in a blur of concentration. Open bomb doors ... check course ... forty seconds ... thirty seconds ... twenty seconds ... steady ... speed – 240 mph ... height – 10 feet ... BOMBS GONE ... now hard on the stick ... clear the wall ... leapfrog the roof.

To French civilians diving for cover, it seemed as if the crazy RAF were trying to ram the prison.

The second wave, 464 Squadron, had a problem. Section leader Bob Iredale got a blunt warning from his

Mosquitoes attacking Amiens prison.

navigator: 'We're bang on time, but the first lot weren't. If we follow them in without a two-minute gap, it won't be healthy.'

Bob knew what he meant. The bombs dropped by 487 Squadron had delayed action fuses – go in too quickly and they might be caught in the blast. Swinging to port, the Aussies began a holding circuit to gain time – a circuit that took them over Amiens-Glisy Luftwaffe base. Dense flak burst around the Mosquitoes and they could see enemy pilots racing for their planes. Circling back over the Albert Road they dropped into the same low-level attack pattern.

To make up for the lost planes, the 464 boys hit the target in two sections of two. Bob and his wingman released their bombs at 12:05 precisely. The last strikes came seconds later from Ian McRitchie and Group Captain Pickard. In those two hectic minutes of combat, the pilots only caught glimpses of the damage they had inflicted. But one disturbing impression came through – the plans had gone awry. 'Black' Smith had watched his bombs smash through the perimeter wall without exploding. The 464 Mossies had seen other unexploded bombs bouncing and skipping in the prison yard. It was clear that the perimeter wall had been far weaker than anyone expected while the bombs, dropped from such a low height, had gone skidding in all directions when they hit thick ice.

Amiens prison wreathed in smoke and dust.

What happened next was up to Pick. The CO had acted as 'Tail-end Charlie' for the mission – the last plane to attack. This was deliberate. With his bombs gone, Pick climbed to 500 ft (150 m) to circle the prison and assess the success of the raid. Through the smoke pall he had to make sense out of the chaos. Hundreds of lives rested on his next decision. Should he call in 21 Squadron to pound the jail – or send them home?

As Pick circled a picture came together. The guards' building had taken a direct hit; the perimeter walls had gaping holes; the main prison had been hit at the junction of the north and west wings. Crucially, dozens of men in what looked like overalls were scampering over the ruins – some of the prisoners at least were out. In spite of the wayward bombs Jericho had worked. Pick's voice came over the RT. He was shouting, 'RED DADDY! RED DADDY!' The others breathed a sigh of relief. This was the signal for 21 Squadron to turn back to Britain.

It was the last anyone heard from poor Pick ...

The Cost

The flight back became a running fight. Fw 190s and Me 109s dived repeatedly on the fleeing Mossies. Most of these screaming assaults were driven off by the escort of Typhoon fighters but others cut their way through. Several Mossies were shot up but gamely they stayed in the air. Then there was the flak. German anti-aircraft gunners were renowned for their accuracy. The dash to the coast became a rat run through dozens of flak batteries.

Ian McRitchie made it to Dieppe, with the Channel in sight, when suddenly his plane lifted in the air like a toy. A gun battery had found his range and kept pumping shells into his stricken plane. He was hit. His navigator sat dead beside him. Ian barely had the strength left to make a crash-landing in a field, where he was quickly captured.

If Pick had a fault it was too much courage. He took chances and expected them to come off. In his adventures fortune really had favoured the brave – but that Friday he let the odds become too high. Once Pick had given the all-clear to 21 Squadron, he should have followed the golden rule: 'Get out of there.' But he didn't. He circled the prison again and again, waiting for the smoke and dust to settle – waiting for a last clear view. By the time he swung F for Freddy away it was too late. Pick was bounced by two of the Abbeville 190s. In a desperate dogfight he mauled one Focke-Wulf badly enough to drive it off. But the other swung in and shot his whole tailplane off. The Mossie flipped over on its back and dived, the impact on hitting the ground scattering wreckage for hundreds of yards. Pick and his navigator, Bill Broadly, died instantly.

In Amiens there was mayhem. Many German guards were dead and over 250 prisoners had escaped. This was better than the Resistance had dared hope for. In the

The damaged prison buildings, looking from a breach
in the west outer wall.

coming months they regrouped and reorganized. When
the invasion force hit the beaches on 6 June the Free
French forces helped to bring the Amiens region to a
standstill.

Yet in war there is no such thing as an easy victory.
Around 40 prisoners were killed in the raid as well as
innocent civilians in nearby houses. A German military
hospital was also hit and over 50 soldiers killed. During
April the Nazis shot 260 survivors of the raid, some
who had not escaped and others who had been recap-
tured. Their bodies were dumped in a mass grave in a
ditch at Arras.

FIGHTING FACTS

The Marvellous Mosquito

Would you like to go to war in an unarmed wooden bomber, held together by glue?

Say that again – UNARMED? WOODEN?? GLUE???

Not keen? Neither was the British government when the de Havilland Aircraft Company first suggested the idea in 1938. 'Stresses from the engines will tear it apart,' experts at the Air Ministry said. Luckily for Britain they soon admitted they were wrong. By the end of the war, 6,710 de Havilland 'Mosquitoes' had been built in the UK, Canada and Australia.

In today's high-tech weapons speak, the Mosquito would be called 'a multi-role combat aircraft'. It became one of the most versatile planes of World War II, serving as a bomber, fighter-bomber, fighter, night-fighter, photo-reconnaissance plane, ship and submarine buster.

'The Wooden Wonder'

RAF crew loved the 'Mossie' and nicknamed it the 'Wooden Wonder'. So what made it so good?

Material

A wooden plane sounds like something from World War I, not World War II. In fact the idea was brilliant. Since the Mosquito was the only all-wooden British plane, it was not in competition with other aircraft for scarce metals, especially aluminium.

Labour

The Mosquito was built by people with woodworking skills – furniture manufacturers, shop fitters, coach and caravan builders. This meant Britain was making good use of all its workers at a time when there was a desperate shortage of labour.

Construction

The fuselage was made in two halves from a sandwich of birch plywood, filled with lightweight balsa wood. This composite construction gave it great strength. The wings were made from overlapping laminated planks of spruce. Many parts were built by small firms all over the country and sent to the de Havilland factories at Hatfield and Leavesden for final assembly. Even better, if a Mosquito crash-landed or was hit by enemy fire, it was easier to repair than a metal plane.

Speed

Although planned as a bomber, the Mosquito was designed like a fighter, to keep drag to a minimum. Lightweight and powered by two Merlin engines the Mossie was as fast as any German piston-engined fighter, even the awesome Fw 190 (see table).

Armament

The bomber version could carry a load up to 4,000 lb (1,814 kg), the same as the much larger Flying Fortress. Remarkably, the bombers carried no weapons. The whole point of the design, de Havilland argued, was to save weight, drag and crew numbers, making the Mosquito fast enough to outrun any trouble.

Fighter-bomber versions, like those in Operation Jericho, were fitted with four .303 machine-guns in the nose and four 20 mm cannon under the cockpit. Fired together, these had the impact of a three-ton truck hitting a brick wall at 50 mph.

Crew

The Mossie only had two crewmen, the pilot and navigator. The navigator had a busy time – as well as guiding the aircraft he had to act as bomb-aimer and radio operator. Smooth teamwork was the key to success. Pilot and navigator often became close friends.

Mosquito vs. Focke-Wulf

Type	Max. Speed	Range	Weapons	Comment
Mosquito FB Mk VI	385 mph (620 kph) at 13,000 ft (3,960 m)	1,650 miles (2,655 km) with 2,000 lb of bombs	Four 20 mm cannon and four .303 inch machine-guns.	The Mossie was a winner in every role it was given.
Focke-Wulf 190 A-5	402 mph (645 kph) at 18,000 ft (5,485 m)	500 miles (805 km)	Two 7.9 mm machine-guns and four 20 mm cannon.	The best German fighter of the war.

VENGEANCE WEAPON

BATTLE BRIEFING

First Strike

On 6 June 1944 Allied armies stormed ashore at Normandy – and Londoners began to relax. For months German air raids had been sporadic and light. Now, with the invasion of Europe underway, it seemed possible that the war might be over by Christmas. This new confidence was rudely shattered at 04.25 on Tuesday, 13 June when the sirens wailed again.

A little earlier, at 04.08, two Observer Corps volunteers at Dymchurch on Romney Marsh watched in amazement as a German missile roared across the sky towards them. They had been warned to look out for a new secret weapon, but it still came as a shock – small, slim and very fast, with a weird engine noise like a 'Model T Ford going up a hill'. They had made the first official sighting of a V1 flying bomb.

No one can be sure if it was the same missile that reached

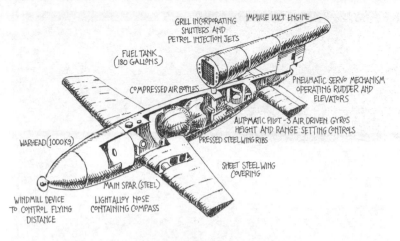

GRILL INCORPORATING
SHUTTERS AND
PETROL INJECTION JETS

IMPULSE DUCT ENGINE

FUEL TANK
(180 GALLONS)

COMPRESSED AIR BOTTLES

PNEUMATIC SERVO MECHANISM
OPERATING RUDDER AND
ELEVATORS

AUTOMATIC PILOT - 3 AIR DRIVEN GYROS
HEIGHT AND RANGE SETTING CONTROLS

PRESSED STEEL WING RIBS

WARHEAD (1000 Kg)

SHEET STEEL WING
COVERING

WINDMILL DEVICE
TO CONTROL FLYING
DISTANCE

MAIN SPAR (STEEL)

LIGHT ALLOY NOSE
CONTAINING COMPASS

A V 1 flying bomb.

London, since four were sighted that dawn. Three crashed harmlessly, but one stuttered to a halt over Bethnal Green.

A ten-year-old girl remembered: 'The engine stopped, then there was the sound of whistling ... and the next thing was a tremendous bang and the front room windows came in.'

She escaped, but six people died and over 200 were made homeless. This was the first of 2,242 V1s to hit London in the coming weeks, killing 5,126 civilians and seriously injuring 14,712.

The V1 was the first of Hitler's high-tech terror weapons, a last gamble to force the British out of the war. The idea to develop a pilotless, jet-engined bomb was given the go-ahead in 1942. It was code-named Fi 103, after the Fiesler aircraft company that was to make the missile. Development took place at the Peenemunde rocket research station on the

One of the first targets,
Lewisham High Street, 1944.

Baltic coast, with the first test launch on 24 December. On 8 November, however, a British spotter plane flying over Peenemunde photographed an experimental launch ramp with a V1 ready for take-off. This was the start of a deadly race between Germany and Britain. The Nazis pushed the V1 programme ahead as quickly as possible while British air raids caused endless delays.

When the first flying bombs were fired at England that invasion summer, they were a year late and RAF Fighter Command was ready and waiting ...

REVENGE!

On 16 April 1944 Joseph Goebbels, Hitler's Minister of **Propaganda**, broadcast to the hard-pressed German people. For those living miserably in the ruins of heavily bombed towns he had a message of hope:

It will not be long before the British will have to show the same steadiness as the Germans. We have the hardest part of the war behind us. England has it still in front of her.

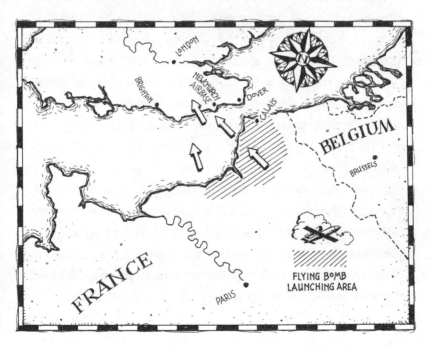

Flight path of the VIs.

Many listeners were puzzled. What did he mean? It was over two years since the glorious days of the Luftwaffe blitz on Britain and six months since Hitler himself had promised revenge for British and American air raids. Was this another worthless Nazi lie, like the boasts about victory at Stalingrad? Or could there be some truth in the rumours of *Vergeltungswaffen* – 'Reprisal weapons'?

Although Goebbels was fit to burst with excitement, the public could not be told how true the gossip was. The first secret weapon, the V1 flying bomb, was almost ready for use. In France over 60 launch sites, hidden in woods across the Pas de Calais, set their target as London. Soon the endless delays and cancellations would be over. Soon these deadly pilotless planes would bring revenge! But would they, the Minister wondered, come in time to save Germany from defeat?

Open Fire

Colonel Max Wachtel, commanding officer of Flak (anti-aircraft) Regiment 155 (W), was one of the men on whom Nazi hopes depended. Goebbels was well aware that this unit had nothing to do with anti-aircraft guns. The title was part of their cover. Flak Regiment 155 (W) was the covert (secret) force that would fire the V1s.

However, Max was a worried man. His concerns had nothing to do with his troops. They were first-class soldiers and engineers who had risked their lives to train with the new weapons. He ruefully remembered that the first VIs had been more likely to explode near their launch ramps than reach their targets. No, his men had proved their skill and courage. But almost everything else continued to go wrong.

Allied bombing had badly disrupted the flying bomb factories. The first missiles should have rolled off the production lines in August 1943, rising to a total of 5,000 bombs a month by April 1944. Instead only a trickle of bombs had been made by February 1944 and barely a thousand left the factories in April. Each bomb carried an 850 kg payload, but in such small numbers they would barely disrupt, let alone smash, a city the size of London.

Equally maddening were the air attacks on the missile sites. The tiny bases were built in remote areas, but even so, British aerial photographs had given most of them away. Once located, the concrete launch ramps, blast walls and blockhouses made distinctive targets.

Preparing a VI for launch.

Since December 1943 Allied bombers had rained explosives on every suspect site from Calais to Dieppe. These raids had cost the British and Americans dear – 154 planes and 771 aircrew were dead or missing by the end of May. But their lives had not been wasted. Eighty-two of Max's 96 launch sites had been knocked out or smashed.

Faced with disaster, Max had risen to the challenge. Repairs were carried out to the damaged bases and new ones begun. What's more, he made sure that there was more than enough construction work to be spotted and bombed! No, he hadn't cracked under the strain. It was all part of a brilliant deception plan.

Elsewhere, hidden from Allied spotter planes in dense woods, smaller sites had been rushed ahead. This time only the foundations were laid, waiting for the last-minute delivery of launch ramp kits. These sites would not become operational until days, or perhaps hours, before they were used. Inevitably a few had been discovered and air raids had ripped them apart, but most remained camouflaged and undamaged. In spite of the odds, by June 1944, Flak Regiment 155 was almost ready to strike back.

Almost, but not quite! On 6 June, the invasion began and Hitler demanded that the VIs be unleashed at once. Germany was now faced with a war on two fronts, the British and Americans in the West and the Russians in the East. Max and his men worked themselves to the point of bleary-eyed exhaustion to obey, but once again enemy air power forced delays. To support the attack in Normandy, Allied bombers blasted anything that moved. Rail and road traffic ground to a halt and with it the supply of VIs, ramps and fuel.

Finally, shortly after 03:30 on 13 June, Flak Regiment 155 opened fire. Each VI roared in anger, locked in the firing trolley to the launch ramp. Then as the jet engine developed sufficient thrust, it was catapulted free and soared into the air. Yet this wasn't the knock-out blow that Max had dreamed of months ago. Instead, only ten flying bombs lifted off and of those only one reached London. Pathetic, but a start! In the coming days the bombardment increased, until by the end of June dozens of VIs were launched each day. As Hitler and Goebbels had vowed, the British faced a new terror.

Tempest in the Skies

If Max and Flak Regiment 155 enjoyed a sense of triumph, it was not to last long. In Britain others were waiting to protect London. In the front line against the flying bombs were the three squadrons of 150 Wing, led by air ace Roland Beamont – 'Bee' to his friends.

Bee had already seen plenty of action. He had fought in the Battle of France and the Battle of Britain in 1940 and flown night-fighters against German bombers in 1941. In 1942–43 he had led daring sweeps over occupied Europe and his attacks on railways earned him a new nickname, 'Train Buster Beamont'. In February 1944 he was appointed Wing Commander of 150 Wing to oversee a special project, re-equipping two squadrons with a top secret plane. This was the sensational Hawker Tempest V. With a top speed of about 435 mph (700 kph) it became the fastest piston-engined fighter of the war below 20,000 ft (6,100 m). Rugged, easy to fly and with a fine gun platform, it was Bee's favourite plane. The Wing was trained and ready just in time to cover the D-Day invasion. And just in time to tackle the VIs.

Bee had chosen Newchurch, on Romney Marsh in Kent, as his Wing base. The airfield was rough and ready, but in the right place, smack in the middle of the flying bomb flight path to London. This was fine for catching VIs, but made life on the ground risky. Shrapnel often rained down over the airfield, puncturing the tents where pilots and ground crew slept. As luck would have it, the unit's first casualty was caused by a friendly plane. A passing P47 Thunderbolt fired on a flying bomb and a stray bullet drilled a hole through the hand of a sleeping airman.

Flying Bomb Battle

On the evening of 15 June, 150 Wing was warned to expect an imminent attack on London. The new German weapon was code-named 'Diver' – a small, pilotless plane, streaking in at 400 mph (640 kph) and at heights of up to 5,000 ft (1,525 m). At dawn the next day the first 'Diver' alert came over the telephone and the Wing scrambled into a grey and drizzly sky.

Soon after take-off radar control directed Bee and his wingman, Bob Cole, to intercept a missile south-east of Folkestone. In spite of clear directions, cloud and sheeting rain cloaked the V1.

'Target is closing rapidly to your port side,' intoned the calm voice of the controller.

Heatedly Bee peered round and pulled his Tempest in a tight turn to port. Where was it? At that moment he glimpsed a small, dark shape flit though a break in the cloud below. The chase was on.

Diving at full power, the Tempests levelled out in hot pursuit of the flying bomb. Bee estimated it was doing about 370 mph but, at 410 mph, he was gaining fast. He looked at it with fascination – a tiny grey monoplane with a glowing, smoke-blackened jet engine at the back. So this was the new face of war? Not the courage and skill of pilot against pilot, instead he was hunting a robot bomb at whirlwind speed.

As they crossed the coast Bee closed in. At 400 yards (365 m) he opened fire with his four 20 mm Hispano cannon – and missed completely. At 300 yards (275 m) he fired again and hit the port wing. No effect! Third time lucky? At 200 yards he raked the fuselage and engine until his ammunition was exhausted. And watched in dismay as the cannon shells seemed to bounce off.

Was the blasted thing invulnerable? Then the engine of the VI cut out and it immediately lost speed.

Thank God! They could be stopped.

Bee called in Bob to finish the job. A long blast from the wingman's cannon rolled the missile on its back. It dived into a field near Maidstone and exploded, a goldfish bowl shock wave rippling outwards.

When they returned to base to refuel and rearm, Bee and Bob reported their kill. Buzzing with excitement they asked if it was the first. Gallingly for 150 Wing, they had been beaten by an hour. A Mosquito night-fighter, flown by Flight Lieutenant Musgrave, had claimed the record. Still, there was no time to be disappointed. Since dawn over 50 VIs had been tracked and more were coming in. Within minutes the pair were scrambled again.

By the end of 16 June the Wing had downed eleven missiles, an amazing achievement against an unknown and sinister enemy. That night, in hectic mission reports, experiences were shared and tactics thrashed out. One thing was clear – these steel-cased VIs were tough nuts to shoot down. Pilots had to get in close.

Guns were re-set so that their fire harmonized (converged or met) 200 yards (182 m) ahead, much nearer than Fighter Command approved. This was risky. No one could be certain that an attacking aircraft would survive if a VI blew up at that range. The answer came the next afternoon when a blackened Tempest landed. The elevators were charred and part of the rudder burned away. The shocked pilot reported:

> The sky was overcast, but there was a big ray of sunshine coming through a hole in the clouds. A VI broke out in front of me. I was right underneath it and let fly for two or three seconds. When I was only 50 yards (15 m) away, it blew up in my face. My wingman saw me disappear in a sheet of flame and shouted, 'You are on fire. Bale out!' I thought I had had it.

Amazingly, both pilot and plane survived.

Soon Bee suffered the same wild ride, 400 mph through the middle of an 850 kg bomb explosion. On 21 June, he described it to an awe-struck reporter:

> You can see the cannon-strikes on the bomb and a few flashes. Then suddenly the whole sky goes black and red and you duck. Everyone who has blown up a winged bomb at short range finds himself on his back when he comes out the other side, probably because the pilot goes through a complete vacuum which turns his aeroplane upside down.

The close kill tactic had been proved a success, but it didn't work every time. In the next six weeks eighteen fighters were badly damaged and six pilots killed when VIs blew up in the air.

Clearing the field

In the coming days other difficulties had to be solved and Bee had firm views about what should happen.

Problem

Radar control could only get fighters to within half a mile (0.8 km) of a flying bomb. After this, detection was down to sharp eyes and luck. Too much time was lost in poor weather.

Solution

Station Observer Corps posts at half-mile intervals along the coast from Eastbourne to Folkestone. Observers to fire distress rockets towards any VI they spot. This will give pilots a useful clue to the direction of the incoming missile.

Problem

Only a handful of aircraft types stood a chance of catching a VI – the Tempest V, Spitfires IX and XIV, Mustang IIIs and Mosquitoes. Yet the skies seemed as busy as at an airshow with too many older and slower planes taking pot-shots at VIs. And getting in the way!

Solution

Ban all other aircraft from the interception area and leave the hunting to the experts – 150 Wing and a few others, like the fearless Poles of 316 'City of Warsaw' Squadron.

Bee flew to Uxbridge, the HQ of No. 11 Group and requested immediate action on these solutions. The

Commander-in-Chief listened carefully and agreed. If he had any doubts they were soon put to rest. With the skies cleared Beamont's boys could get on with the job. The interception rate shot up almost at once.

For the next six weeks 150 Wing fought a hectic battle against the V1s. Pilots flew four or five sorties a day, living and eating by their planes. In normal combat they expected to fly for 500–600 hours a month, but that June and July they were operational for 900–1,000 hours. The pressure was intense and affected ground crews too. The Tempest was a marvellous aircraft, but it was powered by the temperamental Napier Sabre engine. It was common for fitters to work eighteen hours a day to keep the squadrons in the air. Yet in spite of all leave being cancelled, morale was high. The reason was simple – Bee was a fearless and popular leader. Men rose to the challenges he set them.

By early August Wing Commander Beamont's 'personal bag' of V1s stood at 30. Inspired by his example, 150 Wing had destroyed 632 missiles, the top-scoring RAF unit by far. The V1 threat was not over, but the worst had passed. Allied troops began to overrun the launch sites and by early September Flak Unit 155 had pulled back to Holland. London was now out of range of ground-launched flying bombs. It was time for the Tempests to move on to Belgium and the air war in Europe.

FIGHTING FACTS

Every extra mile counts

During V1 tests in Germany, Hitler was shown a dazzling display – a flying bomb easily outrunning a captured Spitfire Mark V. It gave the German leader the impression that the V1 would be unstoppable. But British aircraft technology did not stand still. By June 1944 a number of piston-engined planes, like the Tempest and Spitfire XIV, were fast enough to catch the jet-engined missiles – but only just. Every extra mile per hour that could be teased from them was vital and a number of ingenious modifications were made. Ground crew followed urgent DIY instructions:

How to soup-up your fighter

- Polish all surfaces until as smooth as mirrors to reduce drag.
- Strip off all surplus weight, including layers of paint. V1s can't fire back so remove cockpit armour (usually behind seats to protect pilots from enemy fire).
- Adapt engines to run on 150 octane fuel and increase boost to give extra power.

Although results varied, many planes gained an extra 30 mph (40 kph).

Tip the Wing

On 23 June 1944 a Spitfire pilot tried a new and rash method of dealing with a V1. He flew alongside the missile and according to the official RAF history 'threw the flying bomb on its back by tipping it with his wing so that it fell out of control'. News soon spread and every hot-shot pilot was keen to have a go. One Pole of 316 Squadron successfully flipped the wing of a V1, only to

A Spitfire tips a V1 over.

watch in horror as it rolled back and snapped the end off his own light alloy wing. He made a hasty but safe landing.

Jet vs. Jet

The Germans were ahead of the British in the development of jet engine technology, but only by a narrow margin. In May 1941 the first British test plane, the Gloucester E28/39, was flown and the first operational jet, the Gloucester Meteor, went into service with 616

Squadron in July 1944. The Meteor caught the public imagination and many thought that the flying bomb bombardment was beaten by this new wonder plane. In fact the Meteors arrived too late to make much difference and only shot down thirteen V1s.

Buzz Bombs and Doodlebugs

The jet engine of the V1 had an eerie sound. Once heard it was never forgotten. Witnesses described in different, vivid ways:

- 'a train trundling over a wooden bridge';
- 'a sinister grunting';
- 'a washing machine';
- 'a cough, clattering, like a diesel truck';
- 'a load of biscuit tins rattling'.

This peculiar engine note led to the British nicknames for the V1 – the 'doodlebug' or the 'buzz bomb'.

A Terrifying Silence

The British people soon learned that while a V1 puttered its noisy way across the sky, they were safe. The danger came when the engine cut out. Flying bombs were loaded with only enough fuel to reach their target. When this ran out, the engine failed and the missile dived. Civilians described a 'dreadful silence' that lasted about twelve seconds – the time from the engine stopping to the V1 exploding.

VI Data

- 6,725 VIs reached England.
- 2,242 landed in London.
- 1,444 landed in Kent.
- 1,772 shot down by fighters:
    - 638 by Tempests
    - 428 by Mosquitoes
    - 303 by Spitfire XIVs
    - 232 by Mustangs
    - 158 by slower fighters – Typhoons, Spitfire Vs, IXs or XII.
- 1,460 shot down by anti-aircraft guns.
- 231 were caught by barrage balloons.
- Altogether 51.5 per cent of VIs spotted by the defences were destroyed.
- 6,184 civilians were killed and 17,981 injured.

Mysterious Gas Explosions

Hitler had worse in store for Londoners than the VI. At 18:43 on 8 September 1944 an explosion in Chiswick killed three people. As casualties mounted, a series of mysterious explosions were blamed on leaking gas mains. Such a pretence could not be kept up for long and in November, Winston Churchill admitted Britain was under attack by another German secret weapon, the V2. This time it was unstoppable.

The V2 was the forerunner of today's long range missiles. Powered by a rocket motor it soared up to

The supersonic V2.

110,000 ft (30,000 m), the edge of space, before diving at 3,600 mph (5,780 kph). No aircraft stood a chance of catching one. The V2 carried a 1,145 lb (975 kg) warhead. As many as 1,115 hit England, 517 in the London area, and 2,754 people were killed.

GLOSSARY

Blitzkrieg – 'lightning war'. The coordinated use of
   aircraft, tanks and infantry
Concentration camp – a Nazi prison camp
Dispersal – remote parts of the airfield where the planes
   could be spaced over a wide area in case they were
   attacked from the air
Fuselage – main body of the plane
Luftwaffe – the German air force
Michelin Man – fat rubber man used in tyre adverts
Morale – will to carry on (fighting), general spirits
Morphine – a pain-killing drug
Nacelle – section of the wing structure that held the
   engine
Propaganda – political advertising. Goebbels' job was
   to persuade the German people to accept the Nazi
   government's version of events, through film, radio
   and public speeches

Wingmen – the two pilots on either side of the leader in a V formation

ACKNOWLEDGEMENTS

Imperial War Museum: p.9 CH1170, p.10 C5655, p.18 CH15174, p.19 C1869, p.23 MH13647, p.49 HU35639, p.62 C4973, p.65 CH7774, p.83 C4742 p.88 CH14105, p.92 C4732, p.93 C4734, p.96 C4739, p.102 CH15109, p.105 CL3430, p.109 CH16281, p.117 CL3429

Thanks to George Tones for checking and changing the technical specifications of aircraft performance – a minefield for possible mistakes.

Every effort has been made to trace copyright holders. We would be grateful to hear from any copyright holders not acknowledged here.